Meet Yourself in the Psalms

Meet Yourself in the Psalms

WARREN W. WIERSBE

This book is designed both for the reader's personal enjoyment and profit and for group study. A leaders's guide is available from your local Christian bookstore or from the publisher.

VICTOR BOOKS ®
A DIVISION OF SCRIPTURE PRESS PUBLICATIONS INC.
USA CANADA ENGLAND

Ninth printing, 1989

Most of the Scripture quotations in this book are from the *King James Version.* Other quotations are from the *New American Standard Bible* (NASB), © the Lockman Foundation 1960, 1962, 1963, 1968, 1971, 1972, 1973, 1975, 1977; and the *Holy Bible, New International Version* (NIV), © 1973, 1978, 1984, International Bible Society. Used by permission of Zondervan Bible Publishers; *The Modern Language Bible: The Berkeley Version in Modern English* (MLB), © 1945, 1959, 1969 by Zondervan Publishing House. Used by permission.

Library of Congress Catalog Card Number: 82-62433
ISBN: 0-88207-740-6

Recommended Dewey Decimal Classification: 223.2
Suggested Subject Headings: BIBLE, O.T. PSALMS

VICTOR BOOKS
A division of SP Publications, Inc.
        Wheaton, Illinois 60187

Contents

Preface

If anyone has the idea that the Psalms are only for the weak and fainthearted—because the Psalms are really poems—then let him be reminded that many of them were written by David, king of Israel, one of history's greatest warriors. And let him also be reminded that a good number of David's psalms were written when he was in tight spots as he sought to serve the Lord. The people who wrote the Psalms knew how to turn tragedy into triumph, and that is a lesson we need to learn today. These writers were not sissies!

Because they are poems and hymns, the Psalms must be read with the heart as well as the head. Someone has defined good poetry as "distilled emotion," a definition that certainly applies to the Psalms. You do not read and study the Psalms as you would one of Paul's inspired arguments in the Epistles. When you study the Psalms, you move into the holy of holies where the heart communes with God.

I fell in love with the Psalms many years ago as a seminary student when I heard Dr. Andrew W. Blackwood lecture on "Preaching from the Psalms." Over the years, I have been amazed at the way the Psalms continue to be relevant to modern life, expressing emotions and describing experiences that belong to us today. It is certainly not difficult to meet yourself in the Psalms!

My prayer is that you will not only meet *yourself* in the Psalms, but that you will also meet the Lord, and in meeting Him, find new vision and strength for life and service.

Because the *King James Version* of the Psalms is beautiful and so much a part of our hymnody, I have used it throughout this book. However, for clarification, I have occasionally given my own translation or referred to another translation.

Finally, I have deliberately bypassed some of the "old favorites," simply because they are often preached and studied, and no presentation of mine would say anything new. I have selected psalms that record many different needs and problems in the life of the believer, and I hope that they will help you. If your favorite psalm is missing, perhaps being introduced to a new psalm will compensate for the loss.

"O magnify the Lord with me, and let us exalt His name together" (Ps. 34:3).

Warren W. Wiersbe

1

Let's Just Praise the Lord!

Psalm 145

[1]I will extol Thee, my God, O king; and I will bless Thy name forever and ever. [2]Every day will I bless Thee; and I will praise Thy name forever and ever. [3]Great is the Lord, and greatly to be praised; and His greatness is unsearchable. [4]One generation shall praise Thy works to another, and shall declare Thy mighty acts. [5]I will speak of the glorious honor of Thy majesty, and of Thy wondrous works. [6]And men shall speak of the might of Thy terrible acts, and I will declare Thy greatness. [7]They shall abundantly utter the memory of Thy great goodness, and shall sing of Thy righteousness. [8]The Lord is gracious, and full of compassion; slow to anger, and of great mercy. [9]The Lord is good to all, and His tender mercies are over all His works. [10]All Thy works shall praise Thee, O Lord; and Thy saints shall bless Thee. [11]They shall speak of the glory of Thy kingdom, and talk of Thy power; [12]To make known to the sons of men His mighty acts, and the glorious majesty of His kingdom. [13]Thy kingdom is an everlasting kingdom, and Thy dominion endureth throughout all generations. [14]The Lord upholdeth all that fall, and raiseth up all those that be bowed down. [15]The eyes of all wait upon Thee; and Thou givest them their meat in due season. [16]Thou openest Thine hand, and satisfiest the desire of every living thing. [17]The Lord is righteous in all His ways, and holy in all His works. [18]The Lord is nigh unto all them that call upon Him, to all that call upon Him in truth. [19]He will fulfill the desire of them that

11

fear Him: He also will hear their cry, and will save them. ²⁰The Lord preserveth all them that love Him, but all the wicked will He destroy. ²¹My mouth shall speak the praise of the Lord: and let all flesh bless His holy name forever and ever.

The day some years ago that we took our children to Disneyland, something went wrong with the controls in "Small World," and we heard the theme over and over again as we waited to move out. It was days before I finally got the tune out of my mind!

Some of the psalms are like that: they seem to play the same tune repeatedly. It may be a mournful dirge of sorrow and complaint, or it might be a happy song of victory. Often, the psalms are a mixture of trial, trust, and triumph. The writer begins in a minor key of painful lament, but before he is finished, he moves into a major key of triumphant praise.

Psalm 145 was written with one purpose in mind: to praise the Lord. In fact, the last six psalms in the Psalter are songs of praise, with Psalm 145 as the "introduction" to the series. This special section follows five songs of prayer (Pss. 140–144), because prayer and praise ought always to go together. You will notice that there are no requests and no confessions of sin in Psalm 145. It is pure praise!

Just listen to the psalmist as he speaks to the Lord! "I will extol [exalt] Thee . . . I will bless Thy name. . . . I will bless Thee . . . Iwill praise Thy name" (vv. 1-2). He is not satisfied to wait until he gets to heaven where he will praise God forever. He starts by expressing his praise to God *every day!* Praise is one earthly occupation we will continue in heaven, so we all ought to begin practicing now.

Some Christians praise the Lord and some do not. Perhaps the difference is this: the believers who praise the Lord have their eyes of faith fixed on Him, while the silent saints look only at themselves. When God is the center of your life, you can praise Him every day, because you will always find blessings no matter how difficult your circumstances. To a praising saint, the circumstances of life are a window through which he sees God. To a complaining saint, these same circumstances are only a mirror in which he sees himself. That is why he complains.

What is there about God that motivated the psalmist to praise Him? He found himself caught up in four different aspects of God's person and work.

1. The greatness of God (Psalm 145:3-6)

If God is God at all, He has to be great. Men like to use the word "great" when speaking about themselves, but not much about sinful man is really great. About the only thing God names about man that is great is his wickedness (Gen. 6:5). If you ever get to thinking that God is small and man is great, take time to read Isaiah 40.

GOD IS GREAT IN HIS PERSON (v. 3). Augustine began his famous *Confessions* with Psalm 145:3—"Great is Jehovah! . . ." for he too was lost in the greatness of God. The more you learn about God, and the deeper your relationship grows with Him, the greater He becomes. No one can measure or fully describe His greatness, because it is "unsearchable." The Apostle Paul knew God as few men could know Him, yet he had to confess: "O the depth of the riches both of the wisdom and knowledge of God! How unsearchable are His judgments, and His ways past finding out!" (Rom. 11:33)

GOD IS GREAT IN HIS WORKS (v. 4). Modern man has substituted "laws of nature" or "science" for God, but a believer sees the wisdom and power of God displayed in creation and in history. The history of Israel is a record of the mighty acts of God: the call of Abraham (Gen. 12); the birth of Isaac (Gen. 21); the Exodus (Ex. 12—15); the wonders in the wilderness (Num. 10—15); the crossing of the Jordan and the conquest of the land (Josh.); and the mighty acts of God in delivering His people and establishing the kingdom. How wonderful it is when one generation tells the next generation of the greatness of God's works, as Psalm 145:4 advocates.

GOD IS GREAT IN HIS MAJESTY (v. 5). This word translated "majesty" means "that for which a person is admired and celebrated." The word "glory" is a good equivalent. The glory of God is the sum total of all that God is and does. "Glory" is not a separate attribute of God, because *all* that God is and does is glorious and majestic. God is glorious in His holiness (Ex. 15:11), His work (Ps. 111:3), and His name (1 Chron. 29:13).

The word translated "speak" in verse 5 can also mean "meditate" or "dwell on." Have you ever taken time to meditate on the glory of God? The glory of man is certainly not worth dwelling on, because man's glory is short-lived (1 Peter 1:24-25); but the glory of God is a wonderful theme for meditation.

GOD IS GREAT IN HIS JUDGMENT (v. 6). The "terrible [awe-inspiring] acts" referred to are His mighty acts of judgment. In order to deliver His people, God had to judge their enemies. Passover meant redemption for Israel but ruin for Egypt. Some people so emphasize the love of God that they forget the holiness of God. "For the Lord your God is God of gods, and Lord of lords, a great God, a mighty, and a terrible [awesome]" (Deut. 10:17).

Because the people of Israel were special to God, He defended them and fought for them. He also judged and chastened Israel when the people sinned. Today we need to recapture this "fear of the Lord" that recognizes Him as a God who judges sin. Too often our worship is shallow and sentimental, and our confession of sin is superficial. Could it be that many of us have forgotten the greatness of God's holy judgment?

How can we grow in our appreciation of the greatness of God? By getting to know Him through the Word, and by seeing Him at work in our world. The psalmist saw the greatness of God in a storm (Ps. 29) as well as in the history of His people (Ps. 106).

2. The goodness of God (vv. 7-10)

Greatness without goodness would make God a selfish tyrant; while goodness without greatness would make Him willing to help us but incapable of acting. Whatever God thinks, says, does, plans, and accomplishes is good; because "the Lord is good" (Ps. 100:5). He can never will anything evil for us because He is the giver of every good and perfect gift (James 1:17). In spite of the fact that there is evil in the world, and evil seems to be winning, "the earth is full of the goodness of the Lord" (Ps. 33:5). If this were not true, we could never quote Romans 8:28 and really believe it!

GOD'S GOODNESS IS ABUNDANT (v. 7). "They shall eagerly pour forth the memory of Thy abundant goodness" (literal translation). The picture is that of God's people celebrating the generosity of God. "They shall sing joyfully of Thy righteousness" (literal translation). God does not ration out His goodness like some celestial miser. He shares His goodness—material and spiritual—in a generous way, giving us "richly all things to enjoy" (1 Tim. 6:17).

In His goodness, God gave man dominion over the earth, the privilege of learning God's laws (we call this "science"), and extracting and employing the riches God has placed in the world (Gen. 1:28). But when man broke his fellowship with God, man ceased to be a king and became a slave. Instead of ruling over nature, he is being ruled by his own selfish desires; and as a result man is exploiting nature and wasting that which he should be investing.

In spite of man's failures as a steward of creation, God is still good in His care for creation. He still makes the sun to rise on both the evil and the good, and the rain to fall on the just and the unjust (Matt. 5:45). He is still "abundant in goodness" (Ex. 34:6).

HIS GOODNESS IS COMPASSIONATE (v. 8). He is not good to us because we deserve it, but because He is a merciful and compassionate God. It is when we realize this that our hearts are filled with praise to God. Who are we, that He should be so good to us! Pride is the great enemy of praise.

When we get the idea that God *ought* to bless us, that we *deserve* His blessing, then we can only praise ourselves. We cannot sincerely praise God.

HIS GOODNESS IS UNIVERSAL. (vv. 9-10). In fact, the word "all" is used 13 times in this psalm, evidence that God's blessings are universal. Whether we look through a microscope or a telescope, we see the good hand of God at work. All of nature praises the Creator, with the exception of man; and he has the most to gain by worshiping the Lord!

All of God's works or living things praise Him, whether we hear their hymns or not. "The heavens declare the glory of God; and the firmament showeth His handiwork" (Ps. 19:1). Psalm 19:3 says that the voice of nature is *not* heard, yet the message covers the earth. All of creation is united in a hymn of thanksgiving and praise to the Creator! No wonder David added, "And Thy saints shall bless Thee" (v. 10). As believers, we can join the mighty chorus of praise.

But sometimes it seems that nature is not revealing the goodness of God. We experience devastating storms, volcanic eruptions, earthquakes, and other occurrences that the insurance companies call "acts of God." Yes, sometimes nature praises God in a somber minor key. "Fire, and hail; snow, and vapors; stormy wind fulfilling His word" (Ps. 148:8). Because of man's sins, creation is in bondage, awaiting the return of Jesus Christ (Rom. 8:18-25). The "music of the spheres" will not be in complete harmony until our Lord establishes His righteous kingdom. Meanwhile, God's goodness is still being poured out on His creation and His people, and we have every reason to praise Him.

In fact, it is the goodness of God that should lead sinners to repentance (Rom. 2:4). We often think it is the badness of man that makes people repent, but this is not true. Judas knew he was a bad man, but he went out and committed suicide. When the prodigal son of Jesus' parable realized *how generous and good his father was,* he repented and went home (Luke 15:17-19). As we worship God and praise His goodness, we ought to repent of our own sins and forsake them. How can we sin against such a good and generous God?

The goodness of God also enables us to face life without fear. We sing "This is my Father's world," and it is true. The world is not a prison, built to make us miserable; it is a school in which the Father is training us for glory. Because He is good, all things are working together for good for those who love and obey Him (Rom. 8:28). God goes before us "with the blessings of goodness" (Ps. 21:3). When we look back, we see only "goodness and mercy" (Ps. 23:6). Why should we fret and be afraid when God's goodness goes before us and follows behind us?

"Let Thy saints rejoice in goodness" (2 Chron. 6:41).

3. The government of God (vv. 11-13)

The emphasis here is on God's kingdom, God's righteous rule in this world. Many people have the wrong idea that God is not reigning today, that Satan is in charge of things, and God will not rule until Jesus returns. I have heard sincere teachers say, "In the past, Jesus was the Prophet. Today in heaven, He is the Priest. When He returns, He will be the King." But this is not Bible doctrine.

Jesus Christ is enthroned today (Eph. 1:19-23). "For He [Christ] must reign, till He hath put all enemies under His feet" (1 Cor. 15:25). He is not simply a priest; He is the *King*-Priest after the order of Melchizedek (Heb. 7:1-10). Even though it seems that Satan is in charge, the government of this world is in the hands of God. This does not mean that there will be no future kingdom, when Jesus will reign in glory; for God will fulfill His promises (Matt. 19:27-30). But we need to keep in mind that Jesus is enthroned today, and that He has completely defeated all of our enemies.

GOD'S KINGDOM IS A GLORIOUS KINGDOM (vv. 11-12). The "glorious" kingdoms of men have faded and turned to dust, but the glory of God is everlasting. Because He is a glorious God, He cannot do anything that is not glorious. The great

Xerxes spent 180 days showing his guests "his glorious kingdom" (Es. 1:1-8), but where is that kingdom today? It is described briefly in the Bible and recorded in the pages of dusty history books, but most of the people in the world have never heard of it. Such is the glory of man's kingdoms.

Whatever God does, He does for His glory. Is this selfish and egotistical? Of course not! There is nothing greater than God, so whatever He does must magnify His greatness and glory. For man to act for his own glory is sin; for God to act *other* than for His own glory is impossible.

We certainly cannot understand all of the complexities of God's government in this world. We walk by faith, and often our faith is tested by events and experiences that seem wrong. We must remind ourselves that God is on His throne, and that He is working all things for our good and His glory.

HIS KINGDOM IS A POWERFUL KINGDOM (v. 11). One evidence of God's power is that He is able to accomplish His purposes while still giving to man a measure of freedom. Man's freedom does not deny God's power—it affirms it, for only an omnipotent God could rule and overrule in this world of satanic opposition and human disobedience. His "acts of power" do not violate man's freedom or hinder God's purposes. He is in control!

FINALLY, HIS KINGDOM IS AN ETERNAL KINGDOM (v. 13). What God does will last forever. Today, His kingdom in this world may seem weak and failing; but it will endure long after the kingdoms of men have fallen into ruins. One day, Jesus Christ will "set up a kingdom, which shall never be destroyed" (Dan. 2:44). Only then will the full revelation of His glory and power be exhibited. "The kingdoms of this world are become the kingdoms of our Lord, and of His Christ; and He shall reign forever and ever" (Rev. 11:15).

Today, there is a conflict in the world between the kingdom of God and the kingdom of Satan. When a sinner trusts Christ, he is delivered "from the power of darkness" and is "translated" into the kingdom of God's dear Son (Col. 1:13).

The kingdom of darkness tries desperately to overcome the kingdom of light, but God is the victor. Christ completely vanquished Satan and his hosts when He died on the cross and rose again (Col. 2:14-15). As children in God's family, and subjects in God's kingdom, we share in that victory!

It is worth noting that the *kingdom* idea is an important one in this psalm. In fact, the first verse introduces God as the King. As New Testament Christians, we are prone to forget the kingship of our God, since we emphasize the fatherhood of God and the fact that Jesus is the Saviour. But, He is King! Our Father is King!

4. The grace of God (vv. 14-20)

It is interesting to see how David balanced the seeming contradictory attributes of God in this psalm. He opened extolling the greatness of God, and then turned to the goodness of God. Now we move from God's sovereign government to His sovereign grace! He is a great God on the throne, yet He is a God who is near us, concerned about our needs. The Prophet Isaiah caught this same wonderful balance when he wrote: "For thus saith the high and lofty One that inhabiteth eternity, whose name is Holy, 'I dwell in the high and holy place, with him also that is of a contrite and humble spirit, to revive the spirit of the humble, and to revive the heart of the contrite ones'" (Isa. 57:15).

Our worship must be balanced. If we only exalt God, and extol His greatness and holiness, we may isolate Him from man and his needs. On the other hand, if we fail to exalt Him and recognize that He is "high and holy," we will be prone to bring Him down to our level and treat Him with undue familiarity. The theologians call this the "tension between the transcendence and the immanence of God." Of course, the "tension" is solved by the Incarnation of Jesus Christ; He is "Emmanuel . . . God with us" (Matt. 1:23). Our God is so great, that He is high above us and yet *right with us* at the same time!

GOD IS GRACIOUS TO THOSE WHO FALL (v. 14). He "lifts up all

who fall," and He "raises up" those who are bowed down.
(See Ps. 146:8.) Abraham fell when he doubted God and
fled to Egypt for safety, yet God graciously restored him
(Gen. 12:10—13:4). David fell tragically, yet God raised him
up and forgave him (2 Sam. 11—12; Ps. 51). Peter denied
the Lord three times, yet Jesus restored him and used him
to win many lost souls.

He is gracious when we are bowed down with cares and
responsibilities. "Cast thy burden upon the Lord, and He
shall sustain thee" (Ps. 55:22). "Casting all your care upon
Him; for He careth for you" (1 Peter 5:7). As we worship
Him and wait before Him, He gives us the strength that we
need for the demands of life (Isa. 40:31).

GOD IS GRACIOUS TO THOSE WHO HUNGER (vv. 15-17). The
Jews were agricultural people who depended on the rain
and the soil. God promised to send the rains and to bless
the harvests if they would obey and serve Him. He promised to meet the needs of those who were faithful to Him.
Everything in creation looks expectantly to God for needs
to be met. All of nature depends on Him (see Ps. 104).

How easy it is for God to meet our needs! All He has to
do is open His hand! But how difficult it is for God to get
His people to the place where His gifts are not misused, or
where the gifts take second place to the Giver. "The Lord is
gracious and full of compassion" (v. 8), but His grace cannot promote sin. This is why David mentioned God's holiness in verse 17: whatever God does is righteous and holy,
including His acts of grace.

Grace does not mean that God overlooks or tolerates sin,
like a benign grandfather who smiles at the disobedience of
his grandson. Grace means that God has paid the price for
our sins, that He has upheld His holy Law while at the same
time fulfilling its just requirements. How? In the work of
Jesus Christ on the cross! It was at Calvary that "mercy and
truth are met together," and "righteousness and peace have
kissed each other" (Ps. 85:10). Grace *and truth* come
through Jesus Christ (John 1:17).

If God waited until His people were worthy of His blessings, He would never be able to bless us. Grace means that God gives us what we do not deserve, on the basis of the work of Jesus Christ on the cross. What He gives us, and what He withholds, both reveal His grace and His righteousness. We can never complain about the way God deals with us! (We *do* complain but we shouldn't.) He is far better to us than we deserve.

GOD IS GRACIOUS TO THOSE WHO PRAY (vv. 18-19). David emphasized two aspects of prayer: honesty before God, and the fear of God. To "call upon Him in truth" simply means "to call on Him sincerely." If we want to have revival in our lives, we must begin by being totally honest with God in our praying. But we must not allow this "honesty" to degenerate into undue familiarity; we must "fear Him" and show the proper respect and reverence.

GOD IS GRACIOUS TO THOSE WHO LOVE HIM (vv. 20-21). Our love does not earn God's grace, because grace cannot be earned. Rather, our love strengthens our personal relationship with God, and this deepens our prayer life (John 14:21-24; 15:9-16). God promises to preserve (guard) those who love Him. This does not mean they will be pampered and never face any troubles, but rather that they will escape the sad consequences of disobedience and will receive special help and strength in times of trial and testing.

How strange that in a song of praise, David should mention the judgment of the wicked! But even in His judgments, God is to be praised (see Rev. 19:1-5). The more we love God, the more we ought to hate evil and want to see it judged and destroyed.

David opened this psalm with *personal* praise ("I will extol Thee"), but he closed it by asking "all flesh" to bless God's holy name! And halfway through the psalm, he called on all of creation and all the saints to praise God (v. 10)! What a thrilling privilege we have to praise the Lord!

Let's just praise the Lord together!

2
God Is not Dead

Psalm 115

¹Not unto us, O Lord, not unto us, but unto Thy name give glory, for Thy mercy, and for Thy truth's sake. ²Wherefore should the heathen say, "Where is now their God?" ³But our God is in the heavens; He hath done whatsoever He hath pleased. ⁴Their idols are silver and gold, the work of men's hands. ⁵They have mouths, but they speak not; eyes have they, but they see not. ⁶They have ears, but they hear not; noses have they, but they smell not. ⁷They have hands, but they handle not; feet have they, but they walk not; neither speak they through their throat. ⁸They that make them are like unto them; so is everyone that trusteth in them. ⁹O Israel, trust thou in the Lord: He is their help and their shield. ¹⁰O house of Aaron, trust in the Lord: He is their help and their shield. ¹¹Ye that fear the Lord, trust in the Lord: He is their help and their shield. ¹²The Lord hath been mindful of us: He will bless us; He will bless the house of Israel; He will bless the house of Aaron. ¹³He will bless them that fear the Lord, both small and great. ¹⁴The Lord shall increase you more and more, you and your children. ¹⁵Ye are blessed of the Lord which made heaven and earth. ¹⁶The heaven, even the heavens, are the Lord's, but the earth hath He given to the children of men. ¹⁷The dead praise not the Lord, neither any that go down into silence. ¹⁸But we will bless the Lord from this time forth and for evermore. Praise the Lord.

The "God is dead" movement is dead, and it deserves to be; but that same spirit of unbelief will rise again. Men will always be asking, "Where is your God? Why doesn't He do something?" Those of us who seek to live by faith will always face the challenge, "Prove that your God is alive and real!"

The Jews faced this challenge when they left captivity in Babylon and returned to their land. What a weak and weary group they were! Imagine that feeble crowd trying to restore the temple, rebuild the city, and regain their former glory! No wonder the surrounding Gentile nations laughed at them and mocked their efforts! After all, didn't the victory of Babylon *prove* that the Gentile idols were stronger than the Jewish God, Jehovah?

Psalm 115 was probably written during that difficult period of national restoration, the history of which is given in Ezra and Nehemiah. The writer realized that the contest was not simply between one god and another, but between truth and error, faith and superstition. Today we are not challenged by religious idols, but we are challenged by those who trust their own abilities, or their money, or their pragmatic philosophy of life.

This psalm challenges us to understand what God is really like, and then to respond to Him in the right way. The writer makes four declarations about God, and then invites our response.

1. God is alive—glorify Him! (vv. 1-8)

In spite of conditions existing within the borders of the nation of Israel, God was alive and at work. The temple was in ruin, the city of Jerusalem was a heap of rubble, and the people themselves were demoralized. But the psalmist was giving glory to God! Why? Because of God's mercy and truth. Even the chastening of the nation was evidence that God was true to His Word, and in His wrath He had remembered mercy (Hab. 3:2).

Instead of yielding to the sarcastic taunts of the enemy,

the writer ridiculed their heathen gods. The Prophet Elijah did this on Mt. Carmel (1 Kings 18:27), and other prophets did the same (Isa. 44:9-20; Jer. 10:1-16). The psalmist pointed out first of all that the idols were on earth while the God of Israel was in heaven (v. 3). Furthermore, the idols were not doing anything. They had no will or freedom. Jehovah was free to do whatever He pleased. It was Jehovah—not the Babylonian gods—who brought about the exile of Israel.

He then contrasted the dead idols, made by men, with the living God who made men. As we study these contrasts, we see the blessings that the heathen miss because they do not worship the true and living God.

THEY HAVE NO PROMISES: "They have mouths, but they speak not" (v. 5). Their idols cannot give them any promises! The Hebrew word translated "speak" means "to make articulate sounds, to discourse." The one used in verse 7 ("neither speak they through their throat") means "to make any kind of noise." They cannot make any sound at all! Imagine worshiping a god who cannot communicate with you! Yet, we who trust Jesus Christ and therefore know the true and living God are able to listen to His voice in His Word and commune with Him.

Generally speaking, the gods and goddesses of mythology did not speak to mortal man or give them any promises to claim. The gods of the Romans, Greeks, Babylonians, and Egyptians were distant and unconcerned about the problems and perils of human creatures. But not so with the God and Father of our Lord Jesus Christ! He is love, and it is His desire and delight to speak to us. He speaks to us in His creation and in His Word. He speaks to us finally and completely in His Son (Hebrews 1:1-3). Imagine what it would be like to try to live for God if you had no Saviour, no Scriptures, and no Spirit within to teach you!

THEY HAVE NO PROTECTION: "Eyes have they, but they see not" (v. 5). God's eyes are upon His children, and He watches over them (Ps. 32:8; 1 Peter 3:12). Nothing is hidden from

God's eyes, and He never sleeps. The man who trusts an idol has to watch over the idol; it cannot even watch over itself! (See Judges 6:25-32 for a good example of this.) Our Father sees even when a sparrow falls, and He will watch over His children.

THEY HAVE NO PRAYER: "They have ears, but they hear not" (v. 6). The priests of Baal cried out to their deaf god all day, and he did not hear them (1 Kings 18:26-29). God's ears are open to our cries, and He hears us when we call. In fact, He urges us to call upon Him; He delights in the prayers of His children. It is difficult to imagine what the Christian life would be without believing prayer.

THEY HAVE NO PRAISE: "Noses have they, but they smell not" (v. 6). We realize that our God does not have these physical organs of sense, because God is spirit. The Bible uses human comparisons to explain divine ministries, because this is the only way God could teach us about Himself. "And the Lord smelled a sweet savor" (Gen. 8:21) is the Bible's description of God's response to man's sacrifices of praise. But a dead idol can never receive a sacrifice or respond to worship and praise.

THEY HAVE NO POWER: "They have hands, but they handle not" (v. 7). God's fingers made the universe (Ps. 8:3). His hand is strong and mighty (Ps. 89:13). He bared His arm and showed His strong hand when He delivered Israel from Egypt (Ex. 6:6; 7:1-5). His good hand was upon Ezra (7:6, 9, 28) and Nehemiah (1:10; 2:8, 18). Believers are secure in the Father's hand (John 10:28-29). God stretches forth His hand on the behalf of His people (Acts 4:30).

THEY HAVE NO PRESENCE WITH THEIR FOLLOWERS: "Feet have they, but they walk not" (v. 7). The worshiper must come to the idol; in fact, he must *carry* the idol! "They must be carried, because they cannot walk!" wrote Jeremiah in derision (10:5, NASB). Instead of carrying man's burdens, the false god *is* a burden (Isa. 45:1-7)! But our God goes with us in every situation (Matt. 28:20; Isa. 41:10; Ps. 23:4). Jesus Christ is "Emmanuel . . . God with us" (Matt. 1:23).

What a tremendous thing it is to know the true and living God! Thank God for that day we "turned to God from idols, to serve the living and true God" (1 Thes. 1:9). We are "the children of the living God" (Rom. 9:26) and "the temple of the living God" (2 Cor. 6:16). We are indwelt by "the Spirit of the living God" (2 Cor. 3:3). We belong to "the church of the living God" (1 Tim. 3:15), and are citizens of "the city of the living God" (Heb. 12:22). Hallelujah!

Verse 8 makes it clear that we become like the God we worship. If we worship dead idols (and that could include money, fame, power), then we will die. Actually, since man made the idol, he is really worshiping *himself!* "He is a self-made man," someone said about a vain person, "and he worships his maker." When man refused to glorify God, he ended up glorifying himself (Rom. 1:21ff). Everyone must make a choice: either worship and serve the God who made him, or worship and serve himself. Idolatry of any kind is the glorifying of man and the glorifying of self.

On the other hand, if those of us who do know the living God do not worship and serve Him, we might just as well be worshiping idols! Are we reading His Word and trusting His promises? Are we depending on His protection? Do we pray? Do we praise Him? Are we drawing upon His power and practicing His presence? If not, then we are robbing ourselves of the blessings that belong to those who know the living God.

2. God helps us—trust Him! (vv. 9-11)

It is likely that these verses were sung antiphonally by the temple choirs. One choir would sing, "O Israel, trust thou in the Lord!" and another would answer, "He is their help and their shield." Since He is the living God, He is able to help His people and protect them from their enemies. "God ... is a very present help in trouble" (Ps. 46:1). Our help comes from the Lord, the Creator of heaven and earth (121:2). The man-made idols can never help anyone; therefore, there is no need to fear them.

Three groups are addressed in these verses: the nation of Israel, the house of Aaron, and those that fear the Lord.

At that time in history, the nation of Israel was small and weak. Because of their sin, the people had been chastened by God and sent into captivity. It was their idolatry that caused their fall; but in Babylon, they were cured of their worship of false gods. Their faith in false gods had caused their defeat, but now they are summoned to trust the true and living God and experience victory.

Israel had every reason to trust God. The people knew the record of God's working on behalf of His chosen people. He had built a great nation from a small beginning. He had protected His people in Egypt and then delivered them from bondage. He had cared for them during their 40 years of unbelief in the wilderness. He had triumphantly brought them into the Promised Land and established them in their inheritance. None of His promises had failed.

How prone we are to forget the mercies of God! We see clearly the problems around us, but we fail to look back and see the goodness and mercy that follow us (Ps. 23:6). The great preacher Charles Spurgeon used to say that too often we write our blessings in the sand but engrave our trials in the marble.

The house of Aaron, the priests and Levites, had every reason to trust the Lord. Were they not the servants of the living God? Did they not have the privilege of ministering in His temple and serving at His altar? Were they not the custodians of the Law, with the privilege of teaching that Law to the people? Of all the people in the nation, the priests lived the closest to God's presence as they served in the temple. Surely they would trust Him for provision and protection!

When you read the Books of Ezra and Nehemiah, you should understand how much the people of Israel needed God as their help and shield. The enemies of the Jews did everything they could to stop the rebuilding of the city and the temple. The workers on the wall had to keep a weapon in one hand and their tools in the other, just in case there was a sudden attack (Neh. 4:10-23). But they did not trust their own efforts; their faith was in God, their help and their shield.

The third group addressed—"Ye that fear the Lord"—may refer to Gentile "God-fearers" who often associated with the Jews in their worship. These were people who realized the folly of idolatry and sought to know the living and true God. Paul found the Gentile "God-fearers" a fruitful field for evangelism in his ministry (Acts 13:16; and see 1 Kings 8:41ff). However, we may apply these words to *any* who fear God, Jew or Gentile. Those who "fear the Lord" are those who trust, honor, and obey Him. To those, He will be a help and shield.

This same threefold division of worshipers is found also in Psalm 118:1-4, and a similar one is in Psalm 135:15-21. The latter reference also parallels Psalm 115:4-7, the ridicule of false gods. It is not unusual for various ideas or phrases to be repeated in the psalms and given new meanings in different settings.

The truth we need to lay hold of from this brief section is that God does help us; therefore, we should trust Him. He helps us, not simply because He loves us and wants to come to our aid; but He wants to use this deliverance to bring glory to His name (v. 1). Our experiences in life may be difficult; but if they glorify God, and help us to love and trust Him more, they have accomplished His purposes.

3. God blesses us—fear Him! (vv. 12-16)

Five times in these verses the writer mentioned the blessing of God. What is a blessing really? It is anything from the hand of God that is for our good and His glory, and that we can use in the service of others. At the time, what God gives us may not appear to be a blessing; but if we accept it by faith and seek to use it in His will, it will turn out to be a blessing to us and to others. Note that these verses mention the same three groups named in the previous section: the house of Israel, the house of Aaron, and those who fear the Lord.

God is mindful of His people; He thinks about us. This is a reassuring truth in these days when even the computers forget who we are! "'For I know the plans that I have for you,' declares the Lord, 'plans for welfare and not for calamity to give you a future and a hope'" (Jer. 29:11, NASB). All of God's thoughts toward His children involve their blessing and happiness. We need never fear what the future holds!

While waiting to visit a Christian businessman in downtown Chicago, I sat in the reception room and watched the receptionist as she kept track of a multitude of phone calls. It was remarkable the way she answered the incoming calls, connected them to the proper offices, monitored the intercom, kept an eye on lines held by people waiting to be connected, and managed to give a reassuring word to those of us waiting for appointments. Imagine how much God has to think about as He cares for the needs of His people around the world! Yet He is never a second too late. He never makes a mistake, and He manages everything so that His divine purposes are accomplished.

The fact that God is mindful of us assures us that He never forgets us. The Book of Genesis tells us that God remembered Noah (8:1), Abraham (19:29), Rachel (30:22), and Joseph (42:9). When God makes promises to His people, He always keeps them. "He will ever be mindful of His covenant" (Ps. 111:5). All of this is evidence of His grace. "What is man, that Thou art mindful of him?" (Ps. 8:4) Whether we are small or great, if we fear God and trust in Him, He will be mindful of us and work out His will in our lives.

Verse 14 states the special blessing the nation wanted: an increase of the people in the land. It was important that the nation multiply so that there might be enough workers for the fields and warriors to protect the people. The Jews were but a feeble remnant when they went back to their land. They desperately needed God's blessing to increase in numbers and enable them to reestablish their nation.

Was it selfishness on their part to ask God for the blessing of growth? No, they were concerned for their children, the next generation, as well as for themselves. Remember that the future of the nation also involved *us*, for our Saviour was to be born in Bethlehem, of the tribe of Judah. If the nation failed, then God's plan of salvation would also fail.

He will bless us, not only because He is the God of the covenant, but He is also the God of creation (vv. 15-16). The Bible record of the history of the returned exiles in Palestine indicates that their situation was very difficult. The economic situation was very bad, the crops were poor, and the people had little capital to work with as they tried to establish homes, farms, and businesses. The rich exploited the poor, and the poor cried out to God for help.

The God who created the heaven and the earth is able to provide for His people. This was the argument Jesus used to convince people not to fret and worry (Matt. 6:19-34). "Our God is in the heavens" (v. 3), and the heavens belong to Him (v. 16). Man is God's steward on earth, operating as God's deputy under the mandate originally given at Creation (Gen. 1:26-31). If man is faithful to use creation in the will of God, he will experience God's help and blessing. If he sins and exploits creation, he will suffer the consequences.

God blessed Creation, and God still blesses mankind in and through creation. He gives life and breath to all things (Acts 17:25). He enables lost sinners to enjoy His creation (14:17). It is sad that most people accept and enjoy God's gifts in creation, but worship and serve "the creature rather than the Creator" (Rom. 1:25, NASB).

4. God is worthy—praise Him! (vv. 17-18)

Verse 17 is not denying life after death, or suggesting that the dead exist in some silent realm where they are either mute or asleep. Certainly the full light of revelation about the dead had not yet been given (2 Tim. 1:10), and we must always interpret Old Testament statements in the light of New Testament revelation. But the point the psalmist made is that the dead do not praise God *on the earth.* A dead body *in the grave* cannot give thanks (Ps. 6:5), even though the spirit in God's presence can worship Him. The writer wanted to praise God before men. He wanted to give God the glory while he had opportunity to honor Him before others.

The Lord has blessed us (v. 15), so we will bless the Lord! "Bless the Lord, O my soul, and all that is within me, bless His holy name" (Ps. 103:1). When we bless the Lord, we ascribe honor and glory to Him. We cannot *give* blessing to God in the same way He blesses us, but the love of our hearts and the praise of our lips is a sacrifice to Him that He will accept. In several places in the Psalms, we find the writer blessing the Lord (16:7; 26:12; 34:1; 100:4; 134:2; etc.).

God does not need our blessing, but we need to bless God! We should bless Him for what He is, the living God who meets us in grace and cares for our every need, spiritual and material. As we bless the Lord from submissive and grateful hearts, we grow spiritually; and as we grow, we discover more of His blessings—and we praise Him more! Worship and praise are the thermometer of the spiritual life. If our hearts are cold and complaining, we will be silent, like the dead; but if our hearts are warm and appreciative, we will praise and bless God wherever we are.

In recent years, God's people have been rediscovering the importance of praise. For years, we saw plaques that read PRAYER CHANGES THINGS; but now we see PRAISE CHANGES THINGS. Both are true, because prayer and praise go together. Even when we hurt, in fact, *especially* when we hurt, we need to take our eyes off ourselves and our problems and fix them on the Lord—and praise Him! Praise may not change the circumstances, but it will certainly change *us* and help *us* overcome the circumstances. If anybody had reason to complain, it was Paul and Silas in that Philippian jail (Acts 16:19ff); yet instead of complaining, they praised God—and He delivered them! Our own deliverance may not be as dramatic or miraculous, but it will be just as wonderful and real.

The psalmist saw his praise "from this time forth" as preparation for praise "even for evermore." We had better get accustomed to praise in this life, because we will spend eternity praising God. Worshiping God is one of the few occupations Christians have that will continue in heaven. Psalm 115 ends on the same note that it began—the glory of God. "Not unto us, O Lord, not unto us, but unto Thy name give glory" (v. 1). "Whoso offereth praise glorifieth Me," says the Lord (Ps. 50:23).

William Wilberforce (1759-1833) was one of the truly great Christian statesmen in England. For years he fought against slavery and sought to outlaw it in the British possessions. On March 25, 1807 Parliament passed the bill to abolish the slave trade in the West Indies, the first of several laws that finally ended slavery wherever the British flag flew. Wilberforce's response to this victory was to meditate on Psalm 115:1 and give glory to God!

Where is your God?

Are you trusting in "the living God, who giveth us richly all things to enjoy"? (1 Tim. 6:17)

3
When Good Things Happen To Bad People

Psalm 73

¹*Truly God is good to Israel, even to such as are of a clean heart.* ²*But as for me, my feet were almost gone; my steps had well nigh slipped.* ³*For I was envious at the foolish, when I saw the prosperity of the wicked.* ⁴*For there are no bands in their death; but their strength is firm.* ⁵*They are not in trouble as other men; neither are they plagued like other men.* ⁶*Therefore pride compasseth them about as a chain; violence covereth them as a garment.* ⁷*Their eyes stand out with fatness; they have more than heart could wish.* ⁸*They are corrupt, and speak wickedly concerning oppression; they speak loftily.* ⁹*They set their mouth against the heavens, and their tongue walketh through the earth.* ¹⁰*Therefore his people return hither, and waters of a full cup are wrung out to them.* ¹¹*And they say, "How doth God know? And is there knowledge in the Most High?"* ¹²*Behold, these are the ungodly, who prosper in the world; they increase in riches.* ¹³*Verily I have cleansed my heart in vain, and washed my hands in innocency.* ¹⁴*For all the day long have I been plagued, and chastened every morning.* ¹⁵*If I say, "I will speak thus"; behold, I should offend against the generation of Thy children.* ¹⁶*When I thought to know this, it was too painful for me;* ¹⁷*Until I went into the sanctuary of God; then understood I their end.* ¹⁸*Surely Thou didst set them in slippery places; Thou castedst them down into destruction.* ¹⁹*How are they brought into desolation, as in a moment! They are utterly consumed with terrors.* ²⁰*As a dream when*

one awaketh; so, O Lord, when thou awakest, Thou shalt despise their image. [21]Thus my heart was grieved, and I was pricked in my reins. [22]So foolish was I, and ignorant; I was as a beast before Thee. [23]Nevertheless I am continually with Thee; Thou hast holden me by my right hand. [24]Thou shalt guide me with Thy counsel, and afterward receive me to glory. [25]Whom have I in heaven but Thee? And there is none upon earth that I desire beside Thee. [26]My flesh and my heart faileth; but God is the strength of my heart, and my portion forever. [27]For, lo, they that are far from Thee shall perish; Thou hast destroyed all them that go a-whoring from Thee. [28]But it is good for me to draw near to God; I have put my trust in the Lord God, that I may declare all Thy works.

That saintly French Christian, Madame Guyon, wrote: "In the commencement of the spiritual life, our hardest task is to bear with our neighbor; in its progress, with ourselves; and in its end, with God."

Some of the greatest saints in the Bible had their struggles with God, trying to understand what He was doing in their lives and in the world. You can think of the patriarch Job, or of the Prophets Jeremiah (21:1ff) and Habakkuk. David wrestled with the problem of evil in the world in Psalm 37; and in Psalm 73, Asaph struggled with this age-long question. Why is there evil in the world? Why do bad things happen to good people and good things happen to bad people? Is it really worth it to be a believer?

Of course, some people "solve" the problem by denying that evil exists, but that approach only substitutes illusion for fact. Others go to the opposite extreme and deny that God exists! But then you create a new problem: if there is no God, where does all the *good* come from that we see in the world? Dr. John Hutton summarized their plight when he wrote: "A man who gives up his Christianity only surrenders a life of faith troubled by doubt, for a life of doubt troubled by faith."

You do not solve this problem with an immediate step of faith. It is a struggle. As Matthew Henry put it, the psalmist "got the victory by degrees." As you understand the various stages that the writer went through in his struggle, you will better grasp the solution to this perennial problem of evil in the world.

1. He looks back (v. 1)

The opening verse of the psalm is a great affirmation of faith. The writer looked back on the history of Israel and declared his convictions: God is, and God is good.

He was not an atheist or an agnostic. In fact, it was his *faith* in God that created the problem in the first place! People who eliminate God from the world don't have to worry about the problem of evil. To them, evil is just some temporary by-product in man's evolutionary quest for perfection. Everything is matter; things spiritual never enter the picture.

He believed in God, but he also believed that *God is good.* After all, if God is God at all, He must be perfect; and perfection would include goodness. The history of Israel was a record of the goodness of God, and the writer knew it. God had made a covenant with Israel that He would bless and care for them if they would glorify Him by obeying His Law. The details of this agreement are found especially in the Book of Deuteronomy. However, the writer of Psalm 73 knew that God wanted more than external obedience; He wanted purity of heart. The writer anticipated what our Lord taught in the Sermon on the Mount.

Now, here is where the rub came in: Asaph *was* a faithful Jew, obedient to the Law; and he had a pure heart and clean hands (see v. 13). But he was not enjoying the goodness of God in his life! His godless neighbors were in better shape materially and physically than he was!

What should he do? Was he mistaken in his theology? Was there something wrong with his life that he could not see? (That was the approach Job's friends took when they discussed this problem.) How could he escape this dilemma?

2. He looks around (vv. 2-12)

He was slipping! His standing in his faith was not as secure as before! No matter which way he turned, he was on thin ice. His theological problem was an intense personal problem, and he found himself envious of the wicked people around him.

To begin with, he was envious of their *prosperity* (vv. 3-5). This word suggests "peace and complacency" as well as plenty. Apparently, the psalmist felt that the ungodly don't have the pains and struggles that the godly experience. The ungodly and their children were well-fed, comfortably housed, and successful in this world. They enjoyed good health, while the godly suffered sickness and sometimes didn't have enough money to pay the doctor bills.

Asaph was also upset because of their *pride* (vv. 6-9). If these comfortable people would at least be humble and give God the credit! But, no, they took all the glory to themselves. They wore their pride like a golden chain for everyone to see. They boasted that they had more than their hearts could wish, yet they didn't share any of it with their needy neighbors.

Along with their prosperity and pride, Asaph was envious at their *popularity* (vv. 10-12). The world worships these successful people and runs after them. The worldly crowd that worships wealth and success can hardly wait for the news about their idols! They "drink it all in" and beg for more.

But, where is God in this picture? He is left out completely. "How does God know?" the success-worshipers ask. "And is there knowledge with the Most High?" (v. 11, NASB) "After all," they argue, "we are prospering and increasing in riches in this world, and we are doing it without God's help! We have no need for God."

An attitude like this cuts deeply into the heart of any

devout child of God. How do you answer these people? How do you witness to a world that sees the godless prosper while the godly suffer? Is it really worth it to be a believer?

3. He looks within (vv. 13-15)
In this third stage of his experience, Asaph decided to examine himself and see where he stood. His immediate conclusion was that he had made a big mistake by trusting God and keeping his life clean. "Who shall ascend into the hill of the Lord? Or who shall stand in His holy place? He that hath clean hands, and a pure heart" (Ps. 24:3-4). But the clean hands and pure heart of the psalmist were not bringing him any special blessing from God! The wicked were prospering while he was being plagued! The wicked woke up each morning to comfort while he woke up to chastening!

These were real feelings that Asaph had down inside. He was being honest with himself and with God. He could have piously pretended that he was "living victoriously," but that would have only made him a hypocrite. On the other hand, he did not want to abandon his faith in God, because he knew the truth and could not turn his back on it.

When you have these inner struggles, it is good to talk them over with another believer; but even that has its perils. Asaph was afraid that if he told God's people what he had been thinking and how he really felt, he would cause them to stumble. He did not want to offend the younger saints who had not yet faced some of these deeper problems.

It is an encouragement to me to know that even the great men and women of faith in the Bible, and in church history, had struggles with some of the problems of life. "Wherefore doth the way of the wicked prosper?" Jeremiah asked the Lord. "Wherefore are all they happy that deal very treacherously?" (Jer. 12:1) Job asked the Lord, "Wherefore do the wicked live, become old, yea, are mighty in power?" (Job 21:7) At one point in his successful ministry, George

Matheson, who was blind, had an eclipse of faith. (You know him as the composer of "O Love That Wilt Not Let Me Go.") He frankly shared his problem with his church officers, and they wisely counseled him to wait and give God time. The blind preacher did wait, and God met him with new assurances and strength.

The psalmist is at a critical crossroad in his life. He has looked back and declared his theology: God is, and God is good. He has looked around and become envious at the wicked. His theology did not square with the hard facts of life. He has looked within and found turmoil and unrest, a growing feeling that he had made a mistake and that it was not wise to trust God and obey His Law.

What will he do? Will he abandon his faith and run with the shallow crowd that worships success? Will he try to hold to his faith and pretend that all is well, and all the while deteriorate emotionally and spiritually? Fortunately, he took the right step.

4. He looks up (vv. 16-22)

In spite of his confused mind and pained heart, Asaph went to the temple of God and there presented his case. As valuable as theology is, it can never be a substitute for personal fellowship with God. No matter what we may see in the marketplace of life, we must evaluate it at the throne of God. When we walk by sight, all we can see are the price tags of life; but when we walk by faith, we discover the values. Like the Prophet Isaiah (chap. 6), the psalmist worshiped at the throne of God and there saw God, himself, and his world in a new and different light.

Outlook determines outcome. If we have a worldly instead of a heavenly outlook on life, we will make wrong evalutations and wrong decisions. D.L. Moody and Marshall Field both came to Chicago in 1856. Moody could have prospered in business—as did Field, who became wealthy in the department store business—but Moody heard a call from God and decided to become a Sunday School worker and evangelist. By doing so, he became a blessing to millions around the world. If he had made the wrong decision likely few would remember him.

One of the greatest needs in the church today is for personal and corporate worship. We need to take time to contemplate God, to meditate on His truth, and to express our praise to Him. Worshiping does for the inner man what bathing, eating, resting, and exercising do for the outer man. Some "church services" are too man-centered, and fail to focus on God and His eternal values. Worship helps give vision and perspective to life. It helps us weigh matters and choose the things that matter most.

What did Asaph's visit to the sanctuary do for him? For one thing, it sharpened his vision: he saw the truth about the prosperity of the godless. "Then understood I their end" (v. 17). The important thing about life is not where you are, but where you are going. Asaph saw the future judgment of the wicked: "destruction . . . desolation . . . utterly consumed with terrors" (vv. 18-19). We are reminded of our Lord's question, "For what is a man profited, if he shall gain the whole world, and lose his own soul?" (Matt. 16:26) "Depart from Me, ye cursed, into everlasting fire, prepared for the devil and his angels" (Matt. 25:41).

Psalm 73:20 paints a graphic scene. Asaph sees God as though He were awakening from sleep. He has permitted the godly to prosper and enjoy their sin, but now the time of reckoning has come. "You will despise them as fantasies" (NIV). As far as God is concerned, all of the glamour and glitter of godless people is just so much unreality. There is nothing in it that will last for eternity. The godless live in a dream world, and one day their dreams will turn into nightmares.

But Asaph's worship not only gave him new insight into the destiny of the wicked but also into his own heart and mind (vv. 21-22). He realized that he had been thinking and acting like an animal and not like a believer created in the image of God.

That is the great danger of walking by sight and not by faith: we start thinking like the people of the world. We begin to use a different set of standards in measuring life, and these standards minimize the eternal but emphasize the immediate. We make decisions on the basis of false values, and we get more concerned with making a living than making a life. It is an "animal existence," and it is disappointing in the end no matter how exciting it might be in the process.

Keep in mind that Asaph was not guilty of some gross overt sin. He was guilty of only wrong thinking, but wrong thinking leads to wrong living. If we walk "in the counsel of the ungodly," it will not be long before we stand "in the way of sinners" and sit "in the seat of the scornful" (Ps. 1:1). I am convinced that many professed Christians in our churches are mouthing religious words in worship while at the same time they are thinking like pagans. They do not have a Christian outlook on life.

Now, for the grand climax of Asaph's experience with the Lord!

5. He looks ahead (vv. 23-28)
He has already seen the awful destiny of the godless, but what about his own future? Because he took time to worship God in the sanctuary, he is able to evaluate time in the light of eternity (vv. 23-24). *His present*—"I am continually with Thee." *His past*—"Thou hast held me by my right hand." *His future*—"Thou shalt guide me with Thy counsel, and afterward receive me to glory."

People have the mistaken idea that "eternal life" is simply endless time, an unlimited quantity of years. Eternal life is beyond time; it is the very life of God in the believer *today.* When you trust Jesus Christ, you receive eternal life; so that, for you, heaven has already begun within your own heart. You are living "in time" but enjoying eternity!

God is with us; God is holding us; God is guiding us; and one day, God will usher us into glory. The "afterward" for the godless is eternal destruction, but for the believer, it is eternal glory. The worldly crowd may seem to have an easier time on the road of life, but they are heading in the wrong direction! They are like people lounging in deck chairs on the *Titanic.*

Whenever you feel as though God has not been fair with you, just read these verses and see how rich you are. The unsaved people may have health, wealth, and worldly success; *but they don't have God.* And no matter what you may have, if you don't have God, you don't have anything. The things that money can buy are valuable and enjoyable only if you have the things that money can't buy, and they come only from God.

Asaph was able to evaluate time in the light of eternity and also earth in the light of heaven (vv. 25-26). Earlier in his experience, Asaph had looked at the godless people and said, "They have more than heart could wish!" (v. 7). But now he reverses that conclusion: because he has God, he has everything! To be "heavenly minded" means to look at earth from heaven's point of view. Moses did this when he turned his back on Egypt and identified with God's people (Heb. 11:24-28). To be "worldly minded" means to look at heaven from earth's point of view. Lot did that when he turned away from the vision of the city of God and chose the cities of the plain (Gen. 13).

The ultimate test of life is *death.* We shall die, but we shall have God as our portion forever! Verse 26 is the Old Testament version of Philippians 1:21—"For to me to live is Christ, and to die is gain." It is also a reminder of what missionary martyr Jim Elliot said, "He is no fool to give what he cannot keep, to gain what he cannot lose." *Having the right values is a matter of life and death.* "For, lo, they that are far from Thee shall perish" (v. 27a).

Asaph used an interesting phrase in verse 27 when he described the sin of the godless as "playing the harlot." Worldliness is really "spiritual adultery" (James 4:4-10). Israel was "married" to Jehovah because of His covenant with the nation. When Israel went after idols and the gods of the pagan nations around her, she committed adultery (Jer. 3:6-11; Hosea 1—2; 4:12-19). When Asaph saw the worldly Jews around him going after wealth, possessions, power, and pleasure, he knew it was "spiritual adultery." An idol is anything that takes the place of God in our lives. It is the thing we love, sacrifice for, work for, protect, and cherish. Idolatry means living on substitutes.

The *end* of Asaph's experience is a great contrast to the beginning. He started off with his feet slipping, but he ended standing firmly in the faith. He almost admitted to his friends that his faith in God was a mistake, but he closes his psalm affirming that it was good for him to draw near to God! Instead of declaring his doubts and fears, Asaph ends up declaring God's wonderful works!

Did the situation in the world change? No, *but Asaph changed.* Suppose God *had* reversed things and made Asaph rich and his godless neighbors poor? Would that have solved any problems? No, because then Asaph would not have grown in his own faith. He would still be trusting God *only because God blessed him.* And his godless neighbors would be cursing God just the same!

Psalm 73 teaches us some valuable lessons. To begin with, it encourages us to walk by faith and not by sight. God's Word is true no matter what our circumstances might look like. It also encourages us to get the "long view" of things and not to abandon the eternal for the temporal.

Most of all, Asaph reminds us that we need to spend time with God in worship and spiritual evaluation. We need to live "with eternity's values in view," and this comes from fellowship with the Lord. We do not live by explanations; we live by promises, and God's promises become real to us as we grow in our relationships with Him.

When good things seem to be happening to bad people, don't get envious of the people or critical of God. Just find out what good things God wants to do for His good people—and let Him work!

4
Happiness Is--?

Psalm 126

¹When the Lord turned again the captivity of Zion, we were like them that dream. ²Then was our mouth filled with laughter, and our tongue with singing; then said they among the heathen, "The Lord hath done great things for them." ³The Lord hath done great things for us; whereof we are glad. ⁴Turn again our captivity, O Lord, as the streams in the south. ⁵They that sow in tears shall reap in joy. ⁶He that goeth forth and weepeth, bearing precious seed, shall doubtless come again with rejoicing, bringing his sheaves with him.

Have you ever tried to define happiness? It isn't an easy thing to do! In fact, philosophers have been wrestling with the meaning of happiness for centuries and have really not come to any agreement. It is easier to tell what happiness *is not* than what it is!

The Greek philosopher Aristotle defined happiness as an "activity of the soul in accordance with virtue," but it had to be accompanied by pleasure and provided with sufficient external goods and fair fortune. Chew on that one for awhile! The great Samuel Johnson (who never used a simple word when a jawbreaker was available) said, "Happiness consists in the multiplicity of agreeable consciousness."

Abraham Lincoln was much more down-to-earth in his philosophy. He wrote to a friend: "Do not worry; eat three square meals a day; say your prayers; be courteous to your creditors; keep your digestion good; exercise, go slow and easy. Maybe there are other things your special case requires to make you happy, but, my friend, these I reckon will give you a good life."

Happiness, of course, is a by-product of something else. If you go chasing around, seeking "the bluebird of happiness," you will not find it. We know that happiness does not consist of *things,* because some of the most miserable people in the world have everything money can buy. Nor does happiness come from *pleasures* alone, because some pleasures leave people feeling far worse than before. Augustine wrote, "Happy is he who has all that he desires, provided that he desires nothing amiss." In fact, there are whole schools of philosophy (the Stoics, for instance) who believe that the best way to be happy is to *eliminate* your desires completely! Then you can never be disappointed because you aren't expecting anything anyway!

Psalm 126 is a fervent song of joy. We meet happy people whose mouths are filled with laughter and singing. They are rejoicing, and the people around them are rejoicing. "The Lord hath done great things for us; whereof we are glad!" (v. 3)

But this brief poem does not *define* happiness; it *describes* it in three vivid pictures.

1. Happiness is freedom (vv. 1-3)

The Jewish people were celebrating a great deliverance; "the captivity of Zion" had ended and they were free. We are not told what "captivity" this is, and our first inclination is to assume that the Babylonian Captivity is meant. However, there are good reasons for thinking that the writer did not have the Babylonian captivity in mind.

To begin with, Psalm 126 describes a *sudden* and *surprising* deliverance, which the return from Babylon was not. The Jews knew how long they would be in captivity—70 years (see Jer. 25:11ff, and Dan. 9:2)—so they were not surprised when the edict was given that they could return to their land. Psalm 126 describes people who are experiencing a dream come true; people who have been amazed at God's *sudden* intervention on their behalf.

Secondly, this psalm centers on Zion—the city of Jerusalem—and not on the whole nation of Judah. Apparently there was some kind of attack on Jerusalem that left the inhabitants helpless before their enemies, and then the Lord miraculously delivered them.

Finally, the psalm informs us that the Gentile nations around Jerusalem praised God and rejoiced with the Jews because of their deliverance. This certainly did not happen when the Jews returned to their land after the Captivity! Just the opposite took place: the Gentile nations opposed their return and did all they could to hinder the Jews (see Ezra 4 and Neh. 2:9ff). The Gentiles did not want the temple rebuilt nor the city restored.

Some Old Testament scholars believe that Psalm 126 refers to the time the Lord delivered the city of Jerusalem from the Assyrian army, when Hezekiah was King of Judah. You will find the record in 2 Kings 18—19, 2 Chronicles 32, and Isaiah 36—37. Hezekiah was a godly king who refused to pay tribute to Assyria, so Sennacherib sent his army to Judah to bring Jerusalem into subjection. Godly Hezekiah took the matter to the Lord and the Prophet Isaiah assured him that God would answer. God did answer: 185,000 Assyrian soldiers were slain by God's angel in one night! "And many brought gifts unto the Lord to Jerusalem, and presents to Hezekiah, King of Judah; so that he was magnified in the sight of all nations from thenceforth" (2 Chron. 32:23).

I stood one day in the British Museum in London and studied a six-sided clay prism on which Sennacherib recorded this event. He boasted that King Hezekiah was "shut up like a caged bird in Jerusalem, his royal city." (Ps. 124:7 may be a reference to this.) However, the prism does not record Assyria's defeat! Only the Bible records that.

If Hezekiah's deliverance is the background for Psalm 126, then we can better understand some of the statements. We can imagine the people of Jerusalem in their amazement, "like them that dream." We can also picture the amazement of the nations around them as they beheld God's miraculous intervention on behalf of His people. The references to sowing and reaping are explained by 2 Kings 19:29-30 and 2 Chronicles 32:11. The Assyrians had wasted the land in their invasion, as armies always do, and there was a certain famine on the way. God not only delivered His people but promised to care for them and feed them.

So much for the historical background. What about the spiritual application for God's people today?

Indeed, happiness *is* freedom. There is no joy in bondage and slavery. Yet most of the people in the world think that they are really happy because they are free to enjoy "the pleasures of sin for a season." Consequently, people are enslaved to habits that destroy both mind and body. High-priced entertainers, especially "rock stars," openly boast that they use narcotics. Others are enslaved to alcohol, one of the biggest killers in America today. They think that they are smart, but they are really "foolish . . . disobedient, deceived, enslaved to various lusts and pleasures" (Titus 3:3, NASB).

On the other hand, there are people who would have nothing to do with such gross stupidity, yet they are enslaved to fears that can destroy their lives just as efficiently as can dope or drink. Or perhaps they feel "locked in" as far as their circumstances are concerned. They are in bondage to other people, handicaps, or a hopeless future, and their bondage is just as real as was Hezekiah's in the city of Jerusalem.

The good news of the Gospel is that Jesus Christ can deliver us from all bondage. "And ye shall know the truth,"

He said, "and the truth shall make you free" (John 8:32). "If the Son therefore shall make you free, ye shall be free indeed" (John 8:36). In the first public synagogue sermon He preached, Jesus declared a "year of jubilee" when all the prisoners would be set free (Luke 4:18-19).

When you trust Jesus Christ, He frees you from the guilt and punishment of sin. "There is therefore now no condemnation to them which are in Christ Jesus" (Rom. 8:1). But He also frees us from the bondage of sin's power, so that we can walk in the freedom of our new life (Rom. 6). He sets us free from the fear of death (1 Cor. 15:50-58). He delivers us from the power of Satan (Col. 1:13-14) and enables us to live in victory over temptation (1 Cor. 10:13). We are also free from the Law with all of its demands and judgments (Rom. 7:1-6). The Christian life is one of joyful liberty in the will of God!

How many children and young people have said, "I can hardly wait until I'm old enough to do whatever I want to do!" But being able to do "whatever you want to do" is not necessarily freedom; *it could be the most terrible bondage.* True freedom is doing whatever God wants us to do, because that is what is best for us. We find freedom in obedience, true joy in submission. He did not free us in order to make us rebellious anarchists; He freed us to make us obedient children.

Please keep in mind that freedom in Christ is what enables you to become all that God wants you to become. As you yield to Christ and obey Him, He reproduces Himself in you, and this enables you *to be yourself!* A paradox? Of course— but a blessed paradox! True individuality is the result of surrender to Christ. Cult leaders *duplicate* themselves in their naive followers, who gradually lose their freedom and their individuality. But Jesus Christ *reproduces* Himself in His disciples, who enjoy freedom and individuality in the happy will of God!

Never forget the cost of your freedom: Jesus had to die for your sins on the cross. All God had to do to deliver

Hezekiah was to send one angel to destroy the enemy army. But to save sinners, He had to send His Son to suffer and die. Our freedom is free, but it is not cheap. Therefore, we must not use it selfishly, but for the glory of God.

2. Happiness is fullness (v. 4)

The writer leaves the besieged city and moves to the country; in particular, the area of land known as "the Negev—the south." The word "negev" means "dry," because this was the area south of Israel and near the desert. During the dry season, the riverbeds would be exposed and empty; but when the rains came, the watercourses would be filled and overflowing. Certainly this picture would be meaningful to the people of Jerusalem, since their usual sources of water would be cut off by the Assyrian army. Also, after their deliverance, they would desperately need the rain to enable the crops to grow.

The dry, empty watercourses in the desert are a good picture of our world today. The Prophet Jeremiah conveyed the same idea in a vivid illustration: "For My people have committed two evils; they have forsaken Me, the fountain of living waters, and hewed them out cisterns, broken cisterns, that can hold no water" (Jer. 2:13). Unsaved people are thirsty, but they have turned away from the only source of satisfaction, Jesus Christ—the only One who can give living water (John 4:10ff and 7:37-39).

The great Scottish preacher, Dr. George Morrison, said that "peace was the possession of adequate resources." People with empty hearts can never have peace. But when you yield to Jesus Christ, you experience His fullness. "And of His fullness have all we received, and grace for grace" (John 1:16). The *New International Version* translates this verse, "From the fullness of His grace we have all received one blessing after another." The streams are full! We have adequate resources in Jesus Christ!

Of course, no illustration is perfect; because even nature is not a perfect revelation of God. The fullness of the watercourses depended on the rains, while the fullness that we have in Christ cannot change at all. Our *experience* of His fullness may change, but He does not change. "For it pleased the Father that in Him [Jesus Christ] should all fullness dwell" (Col. 1:19). "For in Him dwelleth all the fullness of the Godhead bodily" (Col. 2:9).

Because we belong to Jesus Christ by faith, and are united to Him, we have access to His fullness. "And ye are complete [made full] in Him" (Col. 2:10). We have within us a "well of living water" that perpetually satisfies (John 4:10-14). More than that, we have a river of living water that flows from Christ to us, and then through us to bless others (John 7:37-39). There is no need for us to drink at the broken cisterns of this world when we have the fresh living water of heaven!

I was having dinner with a widely known evangelist and, as waitresses always do, she asked us if we wanted a drink before our meal. I usually say, "No, thank you" and let it go at that. But my friend looked at the waitress, smiled, and said, "My dear, I took a drink over 20 years ago, and I haven't been thirsty since." And in a very gentle way he gave her his testimony. Here was a man with adequate resources; he did not need the stale, polluted water of this world.

If happiness is fullness, then you and I should experience the fullness of Christ day by day. We need to be filled with the Spirit (Eph. 5:18ff) and filled with the Word of God (Col. 3:16ff). We must be full of faith (Acts 6:5) so that God can use us and answer prayer. If we are yielded, then our lives will be filled with the fruits of righteousness (Phil. 1:11), and we will have "joy unspeakable and full of glory" (1 Peter 1:8).

Before we leave this image of the river, we ought to note another truth: the writer saw their deliverance as only the beginning of greater things to come. It is as though he said, "Lord, you have begun to fill the dry riverbeds with your blessing. Now, keep it up until we are flooded with blessing! You have set us free from the enemy army, but we need to be set free from ourselves and our sins!" He saw in the *physical* deliverance a reminder of the greater *spiritual* deliverance that only faith can bring.

Yes, happiness is fullness. It is not God's will that people have empty lives, or that they live on the sickening substitutes of this world. In Jesus Christ, spiritual fullness is available. God can fill your empty life the way the rains fill the dry riverbeds in the desert, but with this difference: those rivers will one day go dry again, but you can go "from blessing to blessing" as you draw upon the fullness of Jesus Christ.

3. Happiness is fruitfulness (vv. 5-6)

Like any city, Jerusalem depended on the food supplies brought in from the country. Often, when I have driven into Chicago late at night, I have seen the many trucks on the expressways, and at times I have been impatient with them. Then I have reminded myself that the people of Chicago would starve were it not for the truckers bringing in food day by day.

As we have seen, the invading Assyrian army had swept through the land, leaving destruction behind them. God had delivered His people, but what would they eat in order to stay alive? Should they turn their seed into food for today, or plant it and hope for a harvest? No wonder the sowers were weeping as they scattered the seed!

Before examining this important matter of fruitfulness in our lives, we ought to note the contrast between the first half of this psalm and the last half. The deliverance of the city was a sudden miraculous event, but the sending of a harvest is something gradual and natural. It was God *alone* who delivered the city; but if there is going to be a harvest, God needs the help of man. Somebody must plow, sow, water, and reap the harvest. In the first part of Psalm 126, there is singing; but in the last part, there is weeping.

What do these contrasts teach us? For one thing, life is

made up of a variety of experiences from the Lord. There are times when He surprises us by His sudden answers to prayer; while at other times, He makes us wait for the answers, like a farmer patiently awaiting the harvest. Sometimes God does it all alone, and we stand and watch, like people in a thrilling dream. Again, there are times when He expects us to do our part and share in the working. In some events, God works for us; in other events, He works in and through us to accomplish His will.

Wise is that Christian who can discern the way God wants to work. Wiser still is that Christian who realizes that life is balanced, that God works in a variety of ways, and that He will not be fixed by a formula or paralyzed by a precedent. It is so easy for Bible students to imprison God in their own system of doctrine! Then, when God works in a different way, they get upset and question their faith. How much better it would be just to let God be God, and to rejoice at the freedom He has to work as He wills.

Another truth is important: we are delivered so that we might serve. The Jews returned to their fields after Sennacherib's defeat, and they prepared for the harvest. To be sure, the same God who destroyed the enemy could have miraculously provided food; but He chose not to. He summoned His people to serve Him and each other by working in their fields.

The concept of sowing and reaping is found throughout the Bible. It is a fundamental truth of life that "whatsoever a man soweth, that shall he also reap" (Gal. 6:7). It is also a basic principle that we reap *in proportion* as we sow (2 Cor. 9:6-8). As Christians, we ought to be sowing the Word of God into our own hearts and into the hearts of others. We ought to be sowing to the Spirit and not to the flesh. Sad to say, some people are sowing wickedness (Job 4:8), discord (Prov. 6:19), strife (Prov. 16:28), and other evil seeds.

The psalmist reminds us that life is made up of tears and joy. If we sow in tears, we shall one day reap in joy. We may not see the harvest in this life, but one day we shall see the reward of our labors.

But we cannot have a harvest if we sit and do nothing! (See Prov. 24:30-34 for proof that it doesn't pay to be lazy.) We must *go!* And we must remember that *others* are a part of the same harvest ministry (John 4:31-38; 1 Cor. 3:6-9). We must labor *together* in plowing, sowing, watering, and harvesting. There is no competition when it comes to working in God's harvest field!

Sowing is serious business. The sower went forth *weeping,* not laughing. Paul shed many tears over the people in Corinth and in Ephesus. The Prophet Jeremiah prayed that he might be able to weep even more over the needs of his people. Our Lord was "a man of sorrows and acquainted with grief" (Isa. 53:3), and He knew how to weep. If we sow the seed faithfully, and water the seed with our tears and prayers, God will give the harvest. One day we shall rejoice in the Lord as we come to Him "bringing in the sheaves."

A fruitful life is a happy life. It was in a context of teaching about fruitfulness that Jesus said to His disciples, "These things have I spoken unto you, that My joy might remain in you, and that your joy might be full" (John 15:11). For what kind of spiritual fruit is our Lord looking? Souls that we win to Christ (Rom. 1:13); holy lives (Rom. 6:22); our generous gifts to His work (Rom. 15:28); the "fruit of the Spirit"—Christian character (Gal. 5:22-23); and good works (Col. 1:10). Even the songs of praise that come from our lips are fruit for His glory (Heb. 13:15).

Why is a fruitful life a happy life? Because a fruitful Christian is experiencing God's power in his life and fulfilling his greatest potential. Furthermore, he is serving others, and this is a constant source of joy. The more faithful he is to the Lord, the more blessing (and trials) he experiences; but this prepares him to be even more useful to the Lord.

Satan's formula for happiness is that you sow in joy today— do your own thing—but then you will reap in sorrow tomorrow. Sin always begins with pleasure but ends with pain. It begins with "freedom" but ends with terrible bondage. It begins with "fullness" but ends with emptiness and poverty. The prodigal son in Christ's parable is the perfect example of how Satan's formula works.

In Jesus Christ, happiness is *freedom*, the freedom to do His will and become all that He has ordained for you (Eph. 2:10). Satan offers you a false freedom that only leads to slavery.

In Jesus Christ, happiness is *fullness*—a full life of power and service! Satan will offer you fullness, but it comes in a broken cistern that can hold nothing. Soon life will be empty.

In Jesus Christ, happiness is *fruitfulness*—your life making a difference in this world as you labor in God's harvest. Yes, there are tears; but one day those tears will turn to joy when you see in glory what God has accomplished through your life.

Is this the kind of happiness you are experiencing in your life today?

5
Come Clean!

Psalm 32

¹Blessed is he whose transgression is forgiven, whose sin is covered. ²Blessed is the man unto whom the Lord imputeth not iniquity, and in whose spirit there is no guile. ³When I kept silence, my bones waxed old through my roaring all the day long. ⁴For day and night Thy hand was heavy upon me; my moisture is turned into the drought of summer. Selah. ⁵I acknowledged my sin unto Thee, and mine iniquity have I not hid. I said, "I will confess my transgressions unto the Lord"; and Thou forgavest the iniquity of my sin. Selah. ⁶For this shall every one that is godly pray unto Thee in a time when Thou mayest be found; surely in the floods of great waters they shall not come nigh unto him. ⁷Thou art my hiding place; Thou shalt preserve me from trouble; Thou shalt compass me about with songs of deliverance. Selah. ⁸I will instruct thee and teach thee in the way which thou shalt go; I will guide thee with Mine eye. ⁹Be ye not as the horse, or as the mule, which have no understanding; whose mouth must be held in with bit and bridle, lest they come near unto thee. ¹⁰Many sorrows shall be to the wicked; but he that trusteth in the Lord, mercy shall compass him about. ¹¹Be glad in the Lord, and rejoice, ye righteous, and shout for joy, all ye that are upright in heart.

After her beloved Prince Albert died, Queen Victoria lived under a constant cloud of grief and nothing could comfort her. In the evenings, she would weep as a lady-in-waiting read her passages from the Scriptures. One of the ladies dared to try to reason with the monarch.

"Your Majesty, instead of feeling morbid, you should rejoice. One day in heaven you will meet these great people from the Bible—Moses, Jacob, Abraham, Solomon, David—."

"No! No!" interjected Queen Victoria. "I will *not* meet David!"

Queen Victoria died on January 22, 1901 and we have every reason to believe that she met King David and rejoiced at the meeting.

It is unfortunate that the mention of "David" reminds us too often of his sins and not his victories. David was, after all, a man after God's own heart. Most people think of "David and Bathsheba" rather than "David and Goliath." Perhaps this says more about *us* than it does about David!

Psalm 32 is one of the seven "penitential psalms." The others are 6, 38, 51, 102, 130, and 143. Martin Luther called four of these "the Pauline psalms" (32, 51, 30, 143) because they sounded so much like Paul and his teachings on forgiveness and justification by faith. Paul did quote Psalm 32:1-2 in Romans 4:7-8 and made it a pivotal point in his argument for salvation by faith alone.

The tragic background of both Psalm 32 and 51 is David's sin with Bathsheba, his unsuccessful attempts to hide it, and then his confession and God's forgiveness of the king (2 Sam. 11—12). This one event was an ugly blemish on an otherwise faithful life (1 Kings 15:5). After all, David is not the only Bible saint who sinned! Abraham lied about his wife on two different occasions, and his son Isaac did the same; Moses lost his temper; Jacob schemed; and Peter denied the Lord three times. Why pick on David? And (Queen Victoria notwithstanding) God forgave David and one day took him to heaven!

Psalm 32 records the experiences that David went

through as he faced his sins, confessed them, and received God's free forgiveness.

1. The silence of conviction (vv. 1-4)

Although David opens this psalm with a shout of praise, his personal experience began with silence. For almost a year, David hid his sins and tried to avoid facing the consequences. When he could not involve Uriah, Bathsheba's husband, he then arranged to have him killed in battle. The fact that he married Bathsheba and claimed the child as his own, did not make the matter right before God. All the while David was scheming and trying to avoid God, his lips were locked in silence.

David used three different words to describe what he had done. *Transgression* means "rebellion." God had said, "Thou shalt not commit adultery," but David rebelled and disobeyed God. The word translated *sin* means "to miss the mark." *Iniquity* means "to be twisted or crooked." David had rebelled against God and missed the mark because of the crookedness of his inward nature. "In sin did my mother conceive me" (Ps. 51:5). All of us are born with a sinful nature, and that is why we are all sinners.

Instead of facing facts honestly, David began to practice guile and deceit. To his sins of the flesh, he added sins of the spirit (see 2 Cor. 7:1) and only made matters worse. As long as he kept silent and refused to confess his sins, he was under the chastening hand of God. Instead of strength, he had weakness; in fact, he was like an old man with broken bones (see Ps. 51:8). Instead of enjoying strength and "freshness," he was dried up, weak, and without enthusiasm. He was living in a perpetual drought instead of enjoying the showers of God's blessing.

Chastening is God's loving way to bring his rebellious children to repentance. If we humble ourselves under God's hand, He will lift us up (1 Peter 5:6); but if we rebel, He will press us down (see Pss. 38:2-3 and 39:10-11). God chastens us because He loves us (Heb. 12:1-13). He wants us to enjoy the best He has planned for us. Sometimes His chastening includes physical pain and difficult circumstances that only God can change. How foolish it is for us to keep silent when we ought to confess our sins!

"The beginning of understanding is to know thyself a sinner," wrote St. Augustine. He kept a copy of Psalm 32 over his bed and it reminded him each day of his need for God. Had David openly confessed his sins immediately, and not tried to hide them, he would have avoided months of silent agony and divine discipline. There are times when silence is golden, but there are other times when silence is "yellow"— just plain cowardice.

Inwardly, however, David was "roaring all the day long." He was groaning inwardly and feeling the hand of God upon him. This same word is used in Psalm 22:1 to describe some of the sufferings of our Lord on the cross. The Hebrew word describes agony that comes from intense pain. "He that covereth his sins shall not prosper" (Prov. 28:13; and see 1 John 1:5-10).

2. The sob of confession (v. 5)
God sent Nathan the prophet to confront David with his sins, seeking to bring him to sincere repentance (2 Sam. 12). This was not an easy assignment. After all, David was out of fellowship with God and could retaliate in anger. Nathan told a tender story about a ewe lamb (David had been a shepherd in his youth), and the story broke his heart. "Thou art the man!" said Nathan, and David replied, "I have sinned."

Note the repetition of the little word *my* or its equivalent in Psalm 32:5: "my sin . . . mine iniquity . . my transgression." He used the same three words that are found in verses 1 and 2. He admitted to God that it was *he* who had sinned; he did not try to blame someone else. Up to this point, he had been trying to hide his sin; but now he brought it out in the open and confessed it. "He that covereth his sins shall not prosper; but whoso confesseth and forsaketh them shall have mercy" (Prov. 28:13).

What is "confession of sin"? It is much more than simply admitting we have sinned. The Hebrew word means "to acknowledge," while the Greek word (as in 1 John 1:9) means "to say the same thing." These two ideas are joined in Psalm 51:3-4. True confession of sin is not just with the lips, for there must also be a broken heart (Ps. 51:16-17) and a surrendered will. When we confess our sins, we acknowledge that what God says about them is true. We also *judge* our sins (1 Cor. 11:31) and turn from them. What many people think is confession of sin is really only *excusing* sin and looking for a way to escape from the consequences!

If we cover our sins instead of confessing them, then God must continue to chasten us until we submit. The longer we rebel, the more difficulty we will have *after* we have been forgiven, for there is a time of reaping. I once heard the late Dr. William Culbertson preach about the "sad consequences of *forgiven* sins."·God in His grace does forgive us when we sincerely confess our sins, but God in His government must permit us to reap what we have sown.

David certainly reaped a bitter harvest from the seeds he had carelessly sown. The baby died. His son Absalom rebelled and tried to take over the kingdom. His son Amnon violated his half sister Tamar and was murdered by Absalom. David's wives were humiliated publicly by Absalom. Absalom was slain. "Now, therefore, the sword shall never depart from thine house," Nathan said to David; and that word was fulfilled.

How is a righteous God able to forgive guilty sinners? Paul explains this miracle of grace in Romans 4, and he quotes Psalm 32:1-2 as part of his argument. Three words are important: "forgiven," "covered," and "imputed." The word *forgive* means "to lift and carry away." It reminds us of the annual Day of Atonement in the Hebrew calendar (Lev. 16), when the high priest "laid the sins" of the nation on the head of the scapegoat, and the goat was taken away into the wilderness to be seen no more. "Behold the Lamb of God, which taketh away the sin of the world" (John 1:29).

The word *covered* simply means "concealed, out of sight." David tried to cover his own sins with deceit, and yet he was found out. When God covers our sins, *they are gone forever.* "As far as the east is from the west, so far hath He removed our transgressions from us" (Ps. 103:12). The blood of Jesus Christ does not simply cover sin; it cleanses sin (1 John 1:7-9).

The word *impute* is a financial term; it means "to put to one's account." After all, what good is it if, after God wipes the record clean, we sin again; and He starts a new record? David rejoiced because God would never again keep a record of his sins. Paul made it clear in Romans 4 that the person who trusts Jesus Christ is fully and finally forgiven, the record is made clean, and no record will ever be kept of his sins.

How is this possible? Through the wonderful and perfect transaction on Calvary. On the cross, all of our sins were put on Christ's account. He was made sin for us (1 Peter 2:24). And, when we trusted Jesus Christ, *His righteousness was put on our account!* "He [the Father] made Him [the Son] who knew no sin to be sin on our behalf, that we might become the righteousness of God in Him" (2 Cor. 5:21, NASB). This dual transaction makes our forgiveness and salvation possible.

Forgiveness, then, is not cheap, even though it is free. David knew that no amount of expensive sacrifices could take away his sins (Ps. 51:16-17). Our own good works, or even our good intentions, can never solve the sin question. Jesus Christ, the perfect sacrifice, had to die for the sins of the world. It is on the basis of that one perfect sacrifice that God can meet the sinner and forgive his sins.

There is a beautiful illustration of this doctrine of imputation in the little epistle that Paul wrote to his friend Philemon. Onesimus, one of Philemon's slaves, had robbed his master and run away to Rome. There, by the providence of God, he met Paul and was converted. Paul wrote his letter to encourage Philemon to receive Onesimus, forgive him, and give him a new start. Two phrases in the letter illustrate imputation: "Receive him as myself" and "If he hath wronged thee, or oweth thee ought, put that on mine account" (Phile. 1:17-18).

"Put that on my account"—Jesus Christ took our sins and suffered our condemnation. Our spiritual bankruptcy was given to Him!

"Receive him as myself"—Jesus Christ put His righteousness on our account and we are now "accepted in the beloved" (Eph. 1:6).

3. The song of cleansing (vv. 6-7)

There is certainly no joy in the heart of a lost sinner, but those who have been forgiven and accepted in Christ have much to sing about. "Thou shalt compass me about with songs of deliverance" (v. 7), sang David; and he knew something about singing.

Sin in the heart takes singing out of the heart. When David was sulking in his sin and trying to fool God, he lost his joy and his song. (See Pss. 51:8 and 12.) He put his harp on the shelf because he had nothing to sing about. One of the first evidences of broken fellowship with God is this loss of joy. It was when the prodigal son got home and made things right with his father that he experienced joyful fellowship (Luke 15:22-24).

It is interesting to see that David called himself "godly" in verse 6. Do godly people sin and then lie about it? They certainly ought not to do such things, but they do. The word translated *godly* is related to the Hebrew word for "mercy" and "loving-kindness." The godly are those who have, by faith, experienced God's saving mercy and His great loving-kindness. They are godly, not because of who they are or what they have done, but because they have trusted God's mercy and been forgiven. To use New Testament language, they have been "justified by faith." They have a righteous standing before God because His righteousness has been put to their account.

Joy begins with confession, and confession must be made "in a time when Thou mayest be found" (v. 6). This phrase could also be translated "in a time of finding out." There are two suggestions here. First, we must turn to God "while He may be found" (Isa. 55:6) and not presume upon His patience. Hebrews 12:9 makes it clear that we must not trifle with God when He is chastening us.

Second, we should turn to God when we become aware of sin in our life. We must not try to cover sin. Had David immediately confessed his sins to God, he would have saved himself a year of silent anxiety and pain as well as a great deal of chastening. Either we will "find out" our sins or our sins will find us out!

The emphasis in verses 6 and 7 is on God's care for His restored child. As long as David was out of God's will, everything worked against him, and he was in constant danger. But when he confessed his sins and was restored to fellowship with God, David could rejoice in God's protection. This does not mean that God would pamper David and shelter him from difficulties. In fact, David had to endure some heartbreaking problems in the years that followed.

God did not shelter and pamper David, but He did care for him. The waters came in like a flood, but David did not drown. There were troubles on every side, but God was his hiding place. All of this affliction did not tear David down; it built him up! Out of it came some of his greatest songs! David was surrounded by "songs of deliverance" (v. 7). He was protected by praise! No matter where he looked, even in the midst of problems, he saw God and praised Him!

David has come a long way in his experience with God. He began with the silence of conviction, and then came the sob of confession that led to the song of cleansing. He recorded one more experience.

4. The shout of confidence (vv. 8-11)

During his months of disobedience and deceit, David lost his confidence. He was afraid, because he knew he was out of the will of God. It is only when we are walking in the light that we can have confidence with God. Once David was back in the light, forgiven by God, then his confidence returned.

He was confident of *God's guidance* (vv. 8-9). It is God who speaks in these verses, promising to direct His child and accomplish His perfect will. "I will guide thee with Mine eye" (v. 8; also see 1 Peter 3:12). Was God's eye upon David when he sinned? Yes, *but David's eye was not upon God.* God was not to blame for David's wickedness.

Verse 9 suggests that a believer who refuses to obey God actually becomes like an animal. (See Prov. 7:6-23 and Amos 4:1 for other references to this truth. Note too that God compared Saul of Tarsus to a stubborn animal who needed to be goaded—Acts 9:5.) You have two opposite creatures in the horse and mule: the horse wants to bolt ahead while the mule wants to lag stubbornly behind. David rushed ahead into sin, but then he stubbornly held back when it came to confessing his sins.

The warning is clear: if God cannot treat us like children, appealing to our love and understanding, then He must use more severe means—the bit and bridle—to get our attention and control us. "A whip is for the horse, a bridle for the donkey, and a rod for the back of fools" (Prov. 26:3, NASB). Our Father does not want to use the whip, bridle, and rod, but He will use them if we persist in rebelling against His will. He wants to guide us through His Word with His eye upon us. An obedient child should be able to look into his father's eyes and know what his father's desires for him are. All Jesus had to do was look at Peter and Peter repented of his sin (Luke 22:61-62).

David was also confident of *God's grace* (v. 10). Because he was trusting in the Lord, he knew that God's mercy would surround him. On the other hand, many sorrows would surround the wicked. But had not David been wicked? Yes, he had; and sin in the life of a believer is really *worse* than sin in the life of an unbeliever. But God's relationship to a believer is on the basis of grace and mercy, not law. God in His grace gives us what we *don't* deserve and in His mercy doesn't give us what we *do* deserve. David certainly suffered for his sins and reaped what he sowed, but even his suffering brought blessing to him because he trusted God.

When a Christian is tempted, Satan whispers to him, "You can get away with this." Then, when the Christian yields to temptation and sins, Satan shouts, "You will never get away with this!" Satan the accuser goes to work to make the disobedient believer so discouraged and guilty that the child of God wants to give up in despair. I have counseled many Christians who have listened to the devil's accusations instead of God's promises, and they have almost fallen into Satan's insidious trap. (See 2 Cor. 2:1-11.)

It is interesting that there are two basic Hebrew words for mercy. The one used in verse 10 carries the thought of "enduring strength, loyalty." The other word is related to "the womb" and suggests "a mother's compassion." You have the combination of strength and compassion, loyalty and love, in the mercy of God. God's mercy is not something weak. Perhaps "loving-kindness" is a good word to use in describing it.

Finally, David was confident of *God's gladness* (v. 11). "Be glad . . . rejoice . . . shout for joy." What a radical change from the somber silence of those months of rebellion and deceit! But note that the source of his gladness is the Lord and not the new situation in his life. True, he rejoiced that his sin was forgiven (vv. 1-2), but even that blessing came from the Lord. He rejoiced that his guilt was gone and his fellowship with God restored. But David found his greatest joy simply in the Lord Himself. He would have agreed with Paul: "Rejoice in the Lord alway, and again I say, Rejoice" (Phil. 4:4).

An unbeliever reading these words might think that David was a bit arrogant, for in verse 6, he called himself "godly," and in verse 11, he called himself "righteous." But this was a part of David's rejoicing *in the Lord!* It was the Lord who had given him righteousness; it was not something David had achieved himself. Like Abraham, David believed God, and God imputed it to him for righteousness (see Gen. 15:6 and Rom. 4:1-6). It does not honor God for us to say that we trust Him, and then go around under a cloud of guilt. If we have really believed His Word, then we have been declared righteous! Let's shout about it and share the Good News with others!

Apart from Jesus Christ, there is no solution to the problem of sin and guilt and the sad results of sin and guilt in the human life. The psychiatrist can alter the symptoms, but he cannot get to the root cause. Religion can temporarily encourage the emotions, but it can never cleanse the heart. Only Jesus Christ can deal finally and fully with the problem of sin in one's life.

I once visited a lovely young mother who was in the psychiatric ward of the hospital, awaiting special therapy. As we talked, it became clear that she was burdened with guilt from past sin that she had tried to cover. I shared with her the Good News of God's salvation through Christ; she believed, and she was cleansed—and changed! She left the hospital shortly and never had to return; later she became a radiant Christian worker.

Don't sit there in the dark silence. Come and join in the joyous song of cleansing!

6
Uplook for the Downcast

Psalms 42 and 43

¹As the hart panteth after the water brooks, so panteth my soul after Thee, O God. ²My soul thirsteth for God, for the living God; when shall I come and appear before God? ³My tears have been my meat day and night, while they continually say unto me, "Where is thy God?" ⁴When I remember these things, I pour out my soul in me; for I had gone with the multitude, I went with them to the house of God, with the voice of joy and praise, with a multitude that kept holyday. ⁵Why art thou cast down, O my soul? And why art thou disquieted in me? Hope thou in God, for I shall yet praise Him for the help of His countenance. ⁶O my God, my soul is cast down within me, therefore will I remember Thee from the land of Jordan, and of the Hermonites, from the hill Mizar. ⁷Deep calleth unto deep at the noise of Thy waterspouts, all Thy waves and Thy billows are gone over me. ⁸Yet the Lord will command His loving-kindness in the daytime, and in the night His song shall be with me, and my prayer unto the God of my life. ⁹I will say unto God my rock, "Why hast Thou forgotten me? Why go I mourning because of the oppression of the enemy?" ¹⁰As with a sword in my bones, mine enemies reproach me; while they say daily unto me, "Where is thy God?" ¹¹Why art thou cast down, O my soul? And why art thou disquieted within me? Hope thou in God, for I shall yet praise Him, who is the health of my countenance, and my God.

¹Judge me, O God, and plead my cause against an ungodly nation; O deliver me from the deceitful and unjust man. ²For Thou art the God of my strength; why dost Thou cast me off? Why go I mourning because of the oppression of the enemy? ³O send out Thy light and Thy truth, let them lead me; let them bring me unto Thy holy hill, and to Thy tabernacles. ⁴Then will I go unto the altar of God, unto God my exceeding joy; yea, upon the harp will I praise Thee, O God my God. ⁵Why art thou cast down, O my soul? And why art thou disquieted within me? Hope in God, for I shall yet praise Him, who is the health of my countenance, and my God.

Emotional depression has rapidly become a major health problem, not only among adults, but even among children and teenagers. It is reported that there are two thousand suicides a day around the world, and many of these are caused by depression. More than four million people in the United States each year need special medical attention because of severe depression.

In my pastoral ministry, I have learned that even Christians are not immune to this affliction. Our enemy, Satan, wants to discourage us in every way possible; and our having to live in a hostile world does not make the situation easier. Often, discouraged Christians add to their problems by feeling guilty because they are depressed. They need to remember that even great men of God like Moses, Elijah, and Jeremiah had times of discouragement and seeming defeat.

One thing is certain: as Christians, we have divine resources available that the world cannot use or even understand. When unsaved people are discouraged or depressed, they often resort to various means of escape—drugs, alcohol, entertainment—but then discover that they have not really escaped *themselves!* When the show is over, or the "high" is ended, they are worse off than before. Their "escape" only forges another link in the chains that imprison them.

We really do not know who wrote these two very personal psalms, but, whoever he was, he certainly was discouraged! Some students think that David penned these psalms during the time his son Absalom led a revolution against him (2 Sam. 14—18). However, the geography mentioned in Psalm 42:6 does not parallel David's experience, and the word translated "nation" in 43:1 is the usual word for Gentiles. As you read these two psalms, you learn that the writer was being *taunted* by the enemy, "Where is thy God?" (42:3, 10); and this was not David's experience.

It makes little difference who wrote the psalms or what his personal situation was. What is important is that the psalms help point the way to victory over discouragement and depression. From his own experience, the writer says to us, "If you want to overcome depression, then you must make some radical changes in your outlook on life."

1. Stop looking at yourself and start looking at God!

There are 51 personal pronouns in Psalms 42 and 43. The writer uses "I" 14 times, "me" 16 times, and "my" 21 times. He mentions "God" only 20 times, and once he mentions "the Lord." We get the impression that life was a mirror, and the writer was looking only at himself.

Certainly there are various causes for depression, some of them physical, but basically, depression is selfish. You can see this illustrated in the experience of the psalmist. For one thing, he was discouraged because *his plans had not been fulfilled.* He wanted to join the pilgrims in their annual trip to the temple, but he could not go (42:4). When you have eagerly anticipated some event, and have had to change your plans, this can be discouraging. However, who are we that God should *always* work things out to please us? Even when we don't have our way, Romans 8:28 is still in the Bible!

Not only had his plans not been fulfilled, but *his feelings had not been relieved* (42:3). He was "feeding on tears" instead of eating his meals. The enemy was taunting him and nobody was sympathizing with him. (We wonder if the writer had ever sympathized with somebody else in his troubles!) He was surrounded by people, yet he felt very much alone

Furthermore, *his questions had not been answered.* "Why art thou cast down?"/"When shall I come and appear before God?"/"Why hast Thou forgotten me?"/"Why go I mourning?"/"Why dost Thou cast me off?" Then there is the repeated jibe of the enemy, "Where is thy God?" Ten times the psalmist asked "Why?" and we have no record that God ever gave him an answer!

It is easy to see that *self* lies at the heart of the writer's complaint. He wants *his* plans to be fulfilled, *his* feelings improved, *his* questions answered. He is so busy looking at himself that he forgets to look at God! The Prophet Elijah made the same mistake when he fled from Jezebel (1 Kings 19). He thought that the victory on Mt. Carmel would result in national revival, but it did not. "I am not better than my fathers!" he lamented (19:4); and he even asked to die!

While there are times when God's people need to examine themselves and confess their sins, it is a dangerous thing to look at yourself too much. One evidence of this selfish pride (or proud selfishness) is that we see ourselves no matter where we look. This explains why a change in circumstances cannot *of itself* cure depression: we take our hearts with us. The psalmist saw a deer drinking at a brook and yet was reminded of his own yearning for God (Ps. 42:1). He saw and heard the cataracts booming on the river, and thought only of his own deep needs and the fact that he was "drowning" in trials and troubles (42:6-7). Even nature's beauty fails to give peace to the troubled heart, *if* we are thinking only of ourselves and not of others and God.

When our Lord looked at nature, He saw the Father's love and care (Matt. 6:24-34; 10:28-31). The Father cares for the birds, even the little sparrows that fall. He looks after the flowers. The world of nature was a window through which Jesus saw the Father.

Because we are human, it is natural for us to think mainly of ourselves when we are going through difficult times. We must constantly remind ourselves to walk by faith *and to see God in the picture.* After all, God is in control of this universe! "Yet the Lord [Jehovah God] will command His loving-kindness in the daytime, and in the night His song shall be with me, and my prayer unto the God of my life" (42:8). God is in command! We can pray to Him and He will give us a song, even in the night. (See Job 35:10.) The living God is the "God of my life," and I must daily look to Him.

The most important thing about any difficult experience is not *that* we get out of it, but *what* we get out of it. If we are truly thirsting after God, and not just His help and deliverance, then the experience that could tear us down will actually build us up. Instead of complaining, we will be praying and praising God. Life will not be a mirror in which we see only ourselves; it will be a window through which we see God.

2. Stop looking at the past and start looking at the future.

There are two interesting trends in America today: the fascination with science fiction and the growing market for nostalgia. Both these trends are logical: when the present is difficult, people either look to the past or to the future. If we look to the future, we are trying to forget ourselves. If we look to the past, we are usually pitying ourselves; and self-pity is one of life's most destructive forces.

However, not everybody can look to the future with hope. Everybody has some connection with the future, either living or dead. The unsaved have a *dead* connection with the future because they are without hope (Eph. 2:12), but Christians have a *living* connection with the future because they have been "begotten . . . again unto a lively hope by the resurrection of Jesus Christ from the dead" (1 Peter 1:3). A "lively hope" is one that grows and bears fruit. A "dead hope" can only decay and vanish.

There is a right and a wrong use of the past. Moses encouraged Israel to remember their bondage in Egypt lest they become proud and turn away from God (Deut. 5:15; 15:15; 16:12; 24:18, 22). The Passover was an annual reminder of what God had done for them. *When we see God in our past, then the memory will be a blessing.* But when we see *ourselves*, and when we start contrasting our circumstances, then the memory will only bring discouragement. When Ezra laid the foundations of the second temple, the old men wept, but the young men rejoiced (Ezra 3:8-13)! The old men remembered the greatness of Solomon's temple, but the young men saw the hand of God in the building of the new temple.

The past must not be an anchor to hold us back; it must be a rudder to guide us. Philosopher George Santayana wrote, "Those who cannot remember the past are condemned to repeat it" (*Life of Reason,* p. 284). Satan likes to use the past as a weapon to afflict us, as he reminds us of past sins and mistakes. But God wants to use the past as a tool to build us up.

The important thing is not just to remember the past, but to remember *God* in our past (Ps. 42:6). It is helpful to look back and see what God has done. We cannot recapture the past, but we can trust the same God who has never failed or forsaken us. A radio listener sent me a poem that says this perfectly:

> Yesterday God helped me;
> Today He'll do the same.
> How long will this continue?
> FOREVER, praise His name!

The answer to depression is *hope.* Three times, the writer

encouraged himself to "hope in God" (42:5, 11; 43:5). In the Bible, "hope" is not "hope so." The child hopes he will get a new bike for Christmas, but he has no assurance that he will. The hope that a Christian has is a guarantee that the future is secure. Our hope is not in ourselves, or in our circumstances; it is in the living Christ. Four times in these two psalms the writer says that he is "cast down" (42:5, 6, 11; 43:5), but this need not mean that his eyes are downcast. He can look to the future with hope because of his faith in God.

In Psalm 43:1-4, the psalmist lists his hopes. To begin with, he knows that *God will one day defeat the enemy and give victory* (43:1). "Judge me" means "do justice for me." "Shall not the Judge of all the earth do right?" (Gen. 18:25) Sometimes God moves in with great power and deliverance, as He did at the Exodus. But there are other times when He patiently permits His unchanging laws to bring about judgment and salvation. Either way, God gives us hope because deliverance is in our future.

The writer had hope, not only because of God's deliverance but also because of *God's presence and protection* (43:2). Why go around mourning when God is with us to be our strength and stronghold? God may not change the circumstances, but He will enable us to face them and be adequate for them. "O do not pray for easy lives," admonished Phillips Brooks. "Pray to be stronger men. Do not pray for tasks equal to your powers. Pray for powers equal to your tasks" (*Visions and Tasks,* p. 330).

A third source of hope is *God's direction in our lives* (43:3). He gives light in the darkness and leading in the decisions we must make. How easy it is to make wrong decisions when we are under a cloud of depression. In fact, it is unwise to make *any* important decision when we are tired or discouraged, because it will probably be a wrong decision. We must wait on the Lord and trust Him to guide us.

Finally, we have hope because *God is our joy* (43:4). If

we get our joy from our own feelings, or from comfortable circumstances, we will be constantly disappointed. But if we find our joy in Him, in His Word, and His will, then we will experience hope even in the midst of hopeless situations. In Psalm 43:4, the writer says literally, "God is the gladness of my joy." Every joy that we have is made joy because of the gladness God puts into it.

People who are depressed are often living in the past tense. They remember "the good old days" which were really not that good! But people who conquer depression are those who live in the future tense. Like Paul, they say, "Forgetting those things which are behind, and reaching forth unto those things which are before" (Phil. 3:13). They learn from the past, but they live joyfully in the present because they are looking to the future. Their hope in Jesus Christ is "an anchor" that encourages them to move forward by faith (see Heb. 6:18-20).

Each time the psalmist mentioned hope he also mentioned the "help of His [God's] countenance" or "the health of my countenance." Certainly depression and disappointment show on our faces! The thought is that God's face is never marked by disappointment. When He looks upon us, it is with love and mercy. Every Jew knew the "priestly benediction": "The Lord bless thee, and keep thee; the Lord make His face shine upon thee, and be gracious unto thee; the Lord lift up His countenance upon thee, and give thee peace" (Num. 6:24-26). The best solution to disappointment is to see the face of God as He smiles upon us.

There is a vast difference between "When I remember these things" (42:4) and I "will remember Thee [God]" (42:6). To remember the past and forget God is to encourage discouragement! Our only help in the present and hope for the future is God. We must not leave Him out of the picture! It may seem that God has forgotten us (42:7, 9), but we know this cannot be true. Keep in mind that God is much greater than your feelings about Him or your thoughts concerning Him.

A lost world does all it can to manufacture hope, but they have no hope. As Christians, we have a "lively" or living hope (1 Peter 1:3), a blessed hope (Titus 2:13), and a reasonable hope (1 Peter 3:15). It is Jesus Christ who is our hope (Col. 1:27 and 1 Tim. 1:1). Why should we live in the past when we have the assurance of such a thrilling future?

We have considered two changes that must take place in our outlook on life if we are to get victory over depression: we must stop looking at ourselves and start looking at God, and we must stop looking at the past and start looking to the future. There is a third change that is needed.

3. We must stop searching for reasons and start resting on promises.

There are at least 13 questions asked in Psalms 42 and 43. The author asks "Why?" 10 times, and "Why?" is not an easy question to answer. (If you have raised children, you know that!) It is normal for us to ask questions when we are hurting or going through perplexing experiences. *It is not wrong to ask questions of God, but it is wrong to question God.* The Prophet Habakkuk asked God many questions, and God answered him; but his attitude was one of submissive concern and not rebellious complaint.

As you read Psalms 42 and 43, you sense that the writer is getting impatient. Where is God? Why doesn't He do something? When will He start to work? It appears that everything is against him. "All Thy waves and Thy billows are gone over me" (42:7, and see Jonah 2:3).

Suppose God *had* answered all his questions; would that have solved any problems and made him feel any better? No! It is a basic fact of life that *we do not live on explanations; we live on promises.*

For example, if you were to fall down and break a leg, they would take you to the hospital and x-ray the leg and study the break in the bone. On the basis of that study, the doctor would set the broken bone and put your leg in a cast. If the doctor came into your room with the X rays, and carefully explained how the bone was broken and what he did to repair it, would that make you feel any better? Probably not. But, if the doctor said, "You will be out of the cast and walking again in eight weeks!" that would encourage you. We live on promises, not explanations. An explanation may satisfy the curiosity of the mind, but only a promise can heal the hurt in the heart and give strength to the will.

The writer had looked around at nature and seen only himself. Why? Because he was looking for explanations. In his pride and self-pity, he was demanding that God give reasons for what He was doing! Had he looked at nature and watched for assurances of God's promises, he would have found medicine for his aching heart.

GOD PROMISES TO CARE (42:1). After all, if He cares for the creatures of the forest, will He not care for us? "Ye are of more value than many sparrows" (Luke 12:7). "How much then is a man better than a sheep?" (Matt. 12:12)

GOD IS THE LIVING GOD (42:2). We saw some of the significance of this truth in our study of Psalm 115. The enemy might taunt us and suggest that God is dead, or that He does not care; but we know that He is alive and meeting all of our needs *even if we do not see His hand at work.*

GOD PROMISES TO BE FAITHFUL (42:3, 8). The constant round of nature—day and night—is proof of the faithfulness of God. "While the earth remaineth, seedtime and harvest, and cold and heat, and summer and winter, and day and night shall not cease" (Gen. 8:22). Each sunrise and sunset is a reminder of the faithfulness of God.

GOD PROMISES TO FORGIVE AND CLEANSE (42:4 and 43:4). The temple in Israel was evidence that God lived with His people and was there to receive them. The Old Testament Jew had to come with a sacrifice; but in Jesus Christ, we have a final and complete salvation from sin (Heb. 10:1-18). Christians do not have to travel to some "holy place" to find God, because He dwells in us and walks in us (2 Cor. 6:16). We need not go to Jerusalem to worship God, for we worship Him "in spirit and in truth" (John 4:19-24).

GOD PROMISES TO BE OUR STRENGTH AND REFUGE (42:6). The hills and mountains were the strongest and most dependable things the Old Testament Jew knew. "The land of Jordan" would be the lowlands, and the range of Hermon would be the highlands. The Christian life is "a land of hills and valleys" (Deut. 11:11). You cannot have "mountaintop experiences" without valleys in between! But God is a God of both the hills and valleys (1 Kings 20:23, 28). He is our refuge and strength even when the mountains shake (Ps. 46:1-2).

GOD PROMISES TO LEAD US AND RECEIVE US (43:3). It has well been said, "Never doubt in the dark what God has taught you in the light." If we are yielded to Him, He will guide us even when the way seems dark to us. God is working out His purposes, and we do not have to understand all He is doing.

Even if God did give reasons for all His acts, we would not be satisfied. In fact, it would be impossible for us to fully understand all that God is doing! We walk by faith, not by sight—or by explanations.

We have not yet answered the question that the psalmist repeated three times: "Why art thou cast down, O my soul? And why art thou disquieted within me?"

Why are we cast down? *Because we want to be!**

If we will only lay hold of the spiritual resources God makes available to us, we can overcome discouragement and come through triumphantly and glorify God.

If ever anyone had reason to be discouraged, it was Jesus Christ. Truly, all God's waves and billows did go over Him during His "baptism of suffering" on the cross. The enemy was constantly opposing Him, and even His own followers deserted Him. At Calvary, His enemies taunted Him in the same way the psalmist was taunted: "He trusted in God; let Him deliver Him now" (Matt. 27:43).

---

*This statement applies to a Christian who faces the usual kind of discouragement, and not to a person who suffers chronic depression that requires professional care. Some chronic depression has very deep roots and needs special treatment; but even then, the spiritual resources through Christ can help hasten healing.

Yet, our Lord had a "song in the night" (Matt. 26:30) and was able to drink the cup of suffering. He was not thinking of Himself; He was thinking of the Father's will and the needs of a sinful world. He was not looking back but anticipating "the joy that was set before Him" (Heb. 12:2). He did not ask for explanations but rested on the promises of the Father. And He was triumphant!

A friend sent me a short note that said, "When the outlook is grim, try the uplook!"

"Hope thou in God; for I shall yet praise Him" (42:11).

7

The Forgotten "I AM"

Psalm 22

[1]My God, my God, why hast Thou forsaken me? Why art Thou so far from helping me, and from the words of my roaring? [2]O my God, I cry in the daytime, but Thou hearest not; and in the night season, and am not silent. [3]But Thou art holy, O Thou that inhabitest the praises of Israel. [4]Our fathers trusted in Thee; they trusted, and Thou didst deliver them. [5]They cried unto Thee, and were delivered; they trusted in Thee, and were not confounded. [6]But I am a worm, and no man; a reproach of men, and despised of the people. [7]All they that see me laugh me to scorn; they shoot out the lip, they shake the head, saying, [8]"He trusted on the Lord that He would deliver him; let Him deliver him, seeing he delighted in Him." [9]But Thou art He that took me out of the womb; Thou didst make me hope when I was upon my mother's breasts. [10]I was cast upon Thee from the womb; Thou art my God from my mother's belly. [11]Be not far from me; for trouble is near; for there is none to help. [12]Many bulls have compassed me; strong bulls of Bashan have beset me round. [13]They gaped upon me with their mouths, as a ravening and a roaring lion. [14]I am poured out like water, and all my bones are out of joint; my heart is like wax; it is melted in the midst of my bowels. [15]My strength is dried up like a potsherd; and my tongue cleaveth to my jaws; and Thou hast brought me into the dust of death. [16]For dogs have compassed me, the assembly of the wicked have enclosed me; they pierced my hands and my feet. [17]I may

tell all my bones: they look and stare upon me. [18]They part my garments among them, and cast lots upon my vesture. [19]But be not Thou far from me, O Lord; O my strength, haste Thee to help me. [20]Deliver my soul from the sword; my darling from the power of the dog. [21]Save me from the lion's mouth; for Thou hast heard me from the horns of the unicorns. [22]I will declare Thy name unto my brethren; in the midst of the congregation will I praise Thee. [23]Ye that fear the Lord, praise Him; all ye the seed of Jacob, glorify Him; and fear Him, all ye the seed of Israel. [24]For He hath not despised nor abhorred the affliction of the afflicted; neither hath He hid His face from him; but when he cried unto Him, He heard. [25]My praise shall be of Thee in the great congregation; I will pay my vows before them that fear Him. [26]The meek shall eat and be satisfied; they shall praise the Lord that seek Him; your heart shall live forever. [27]All the ends of the world shall remember and turn unto the Lord, and all the kindreds of the nations shall worship before Thee. [28]For the kingdom is the Lord's, and He is the governor among the nations. [29]All they that be fat upon earth shall eat and worship, all they that go down to the dust shall bow before Him, and none can keep alive his own soul. [30]A seed shall serve Him; it shall be accounted to the Lord for a generation. [31]They shall come, and shall declare His righteousness unto a people that shall be born, that He hath done this.

It is embarrassing to find yourself in an unfamiliar church, singing the wrong words to a familiar hymn! The hymn was "Alas, and Did My Saviour Bleed," and the words I sang were:

"Would He devote that sacred head
For such a worm as I?"

But everybody else was singing:

"Would He devote that sacred head
For sinners such as I?"

I felt like nudging my wife and saying, "We aren't worms anymore! We're just plain sinners!"

However, our Lord did not hesitate to call Himself a worm. "But I am a worm, and no man," He said in Psalm 22:6. We remember all the other "I Am" statements that He made, but we forget this one. He had to become "a worm" because He took our place on the cross, *and we are worms!*

Psalm 22 is one of the great messianic psalms. Those who deny the inspiration of the Bible and/or the deity of Christ try hard to rob this psalm of its prophetic character. Some say it is only an expression of some kind of intense suffering that David endured. But we have no record that David ever endured this kind of rejection, scorn, and violence. David is the author of the psalm, and David was a prophet (Acts 2:29-30). He wrote about the Lord Jesus Christ!

Actually, Psalms 22, 23, and 24 (all of them by David) belong together, because they describe the "shepherd" ministries of Jesus Christ. In Psalm 22, He is the Good Shepherd who dies for the sheep (see John 10:1-18); in Psalm 23, He is the Great Shepherd who lives for the sheep and cares for them (Heb. 13:20-21); and in Psalm 24, He is the Chief Shepherd who comes for the sheep to take them to glory (1 Peter 5:4). Since David himself was a shepherd, it was only proper that he write these prophetic "shepherd psalms" about the coming Messiah.

The psalm describes two aspects of our Lord's ministry, as stated in 1 Peter 1:11: "the sufferings of Christ, and the glory that should follow."

1. Suffering: the rejected Saviour (vv. 1-21)

Before we study the three different kinds of suffering that our Lord endured at Calvary, we must note the special way that this first section of the psalm is put together. The writer speaks about himself, and then he speaks about God. He speaks about himself in verses 1-2, 6-8, and 11-18; and he speaks about God (or to God) in verses 3-5, 9-10, and 19-

21. No matter how difficult his situation might be, the writer keeps God before him and seeks to relate his own needs to God's abundant provision.

Perhaps there is a basic principle here for us to understand and apply in our own times of suffering and trial. If we look only at ourselves, we will be tempted to drown in an ever-deepening self-pity. But if we look only at God, we may lose touch with reality. Evangelist D.L. Moody used to warn Christians not to be "so heavenly minded that they are no earthly good." When we see a need in our own lives, we must look by faith to Christ and match His adequacy with that need. Then that need can become a strength for serving God and glorifying Him. (See 2 Cor. 12:7-10.)

A. FORSAKEN BY THE FATHER (vv. 1-5). Jesus quoted verse 1 on the cross (Matt. 27:46; Mark 15:34). He cried these words at the ninth hour (3 P.M.) at the close of a three-hour period of darkness. In verse 2, we may have a suggestion of the alternate periods of light and darkness ("daytime . . . night season").

That the Son of God should be forsaken by His Father is a mystery too profound for us to understand or explain. We are not surprised that the disciples would forsake Him, for they were weak and sinful men (Matt. 26:56). But Jesus had affirmed the Father's presence with Him, even though the disciples would fail Him (John 16:32). Now it would appear that even the Father had left Him alone!

In one sense, the Father never forsakes any man, for "in Him we live, and move, and have our being" (Acts 17:28). If the Father forsook any of us for even one second, we would perish! "He giveth to all life, and breath, and all things" (17:25). The breath in our lips and the blood circulating in our bodies—both depend on God for success in keeping us alive.

Verses 3-5 help us understand a small measure of what was involved in our Lord's being forsaken on the cross. One factor is *the holiness of God.* When Jesus Christ became a curse for us (Gal. 3:13) and was "made sin" (2 Cor. 5:21), the

Father for that instant, as it were, rejected His own beloved Son. What a paradox that our holy God had to forsake His Son in order to reconcile lost sinners to Himself!

Another factor is *the glory of God.* God is "enthroned on the praises of Israel" (v. 3, NIV margin). The mercy seat on the ark in the holy of holies in the temple (or tabernacle) was the very throne of God, and it was there that God's glory dwelt (Ex. 40:34ff). Our salvation, purchased by the blood of Christ, has for its ultimate aim the eternal glory of God (Eph. 1:6, 12, 14). Out of the darkness of Calvary came glory to the Father!

A third factor is *the character of God* (vv. 4-5). God has always been faithful to His people, maintained His covenant, and kept His promises. When you read Old Testament history, you see clearly that God cared for His people and answered their cries. From a human point of view, it appeared that God *had* abandoned His Son; but this proved to be a false conclusion. God's character was at stake! If the Father had permanently turned away from His Son, the Father's own character would have been open to attack. Of course, such a thing is unthinkable and impossible, for then God would cease to be God. This long section on suffering begins with "but Thou hearest not" (see v. 2), but it ends with "Thou hast heard me" (see v. 21).

B. DESPISED BY THE PEOPLE (vv. 6-10). Our Lord was not treated like a human being; He was treated like a worm! As far as His nation was concerned, He was "no man." They rejected Him socially, for they called Him a drunkard and a friend of sinners (Matt. 11:19). He was denied His legal rights, for He was arrested and tried illegally and considered guilty before the case was even heard! The officials who should have guaranteed a fair trial actually hired false witnesses!

They treated Him brutally, subjecting Him to all kinds of humiliation and physical pain. While He was suffering on the cross, they ridiculed Him even more! (See Matt. 27:39-

43; Mark 15:29-32; and Luke 23:35-37.) You would think that His enemies would have at least permitted Him to die in peace, but so wicked is the human heart that it must give full vent to its hatred of God as long as it has opportunity.

There is a false logic expressed in verse 8: "If you live by faith, then God must always deliver you from trouble." Job's friends argued this case and were wrong. There is no contradiction or conflict between God's love and human suffering in the will of God. Jesus Christ was doing the Father's will, and the Father loved Him; yet Jesus was suffering. He was not delivered *from* suffering, but He was delivered *through* suffering, and He transformed that suffering into glory.

In verses 9-10, our Lord turned to His Father, just as He had done in verse 3. He reminded the Father that His birth into the world had been a part of the Father's plan. Satan had tried to prevent Jesus from being born into the world, but he had failed. Then Satan had tried to slay the infant Jesus, but again had failed. The Father had cared for the Son in the past, *and He was still caring for Him.* In verses 4-5, our Lord reminded the Father of the Father's care of the nation of Israel; but here the emphasis is on the Father's care for His Son. Even in the midst of suffering, the Son knew He could trust the Father.

C. CRUCIFIED! (vv. 11-21) This long section is a graphic picture of death by crucifixion. The fact that such a description is found here is amazing, because the Jews did not practice crucifixion. This horrible form of death was devised by the Medes, Persians, and Assyrians, from whom it spread throughout the East. The Romans borrowed it from the Phoenicians. The closest thing Israel had to crucifixion was the hanging of a *dead* body on a tree as a final act of humiliation. (See Deut. 21:22-23 and Gal. 3:13). This vivid description of crucifixion is another evidence of the divine inspiration of the Bible, for what would David have known about this Gentile custom?

The picture is one of base brutality. Note that the comparisons given are all related to *beasts:* bulls, the lion (vv. 13 and 21), dogs (vv. 16 and 20), and wild oxen (v. 21, NIV). When men reject God's truth, they become like beasts! (We touched on this in our study of Psalm 32.) Just imagine all of these bloodthirsty beasts surrounding a little worm!

The Gospel record of the Crucifixion (unlike much evangelistic preaching) does not emphasize the *physical* suffering of our Lord on the cross. Thousands of people were crucified by the Romans, and each victim felt the agonizing pain. The important thing about our Lord's death was not the physical agony so much as the *spiritual* agony of being made sin for us and being separated from the Father. However, it is good for us to know how much He did suffer for us, for our sins helped to put Him on the cross.

Verse 14 describes the ebbing strength of the Saviour on the cross. It is worth noting that His bones were not *broken,* even though they felt like they were out of joint (John 19:31-37; Ex. 12:46). "He was crucified through weakness" (2 Cor. 13:4).

Psalm 22:15 speaks of the terrible thirst that the victims always felt. Our Lord said, "I thirst" and thus fulfilled Scripture (John 19:28-30). He who freely gives us the water of life, Himself thirsted on the cross.

"They pierced My hands and My feet" (v. 16) certainly describes crucifixion! Jesus used the wounds in His hands and feet to prove that it was really He who appeared to the disciples (Luke 24:36-40; John 20:24-29). Some of our hymns speak about "scars," but the Scriptures use the word "print," which simply means "the mark made by a blow." Our Lord has these marks in heaven today! When He comes again, He will be recognized by Israel because of these prints (Zech. 12:10; John 19:37).

Psalm 22:17 states the shameful fact that our Lord was publicly exposed before the people who went by. He was crucified at a busy place outside Jerusalem, and the crowd that went past was so cosmopolitan that Pilate's inscription on the cross had to be in three different languages!

Matthew 27:35 and John 19:24 record the fulfillment of Psalm 22:18. Our Lord had no "earthly goods" to leave to anyone, since He was a poor man. Of course, the spiritual riches that we have because of Calvary are far too great to calculate. It was customary for the four Roman soldiers who were in charge to share whatever goods they could get from their victims. There were five parts to our Lord's garments, so each soldier got one item; and they cast lots again for the seamless robe.

You will want to read the cries recorded in verses 19-21 in the light of Hebrews 5:7. Jesus did not pray to be delivered *from* death, because He came to earth to die. He prayed to be delivered *out of* death; that is, He prayed for resurrection. The Father answered that prayer and raised Him from the dead on the third day. The phrase "my darling" in verse 20 means "my only one," that is, "my precious life." The word "unicorns" in the *King James Version* of verse 21 should read "wild oxen." Unicorns are mythical creatures.

As you meditate on these first 21 verses, you cannot help but be amazed that the Son of God would endure all of this for lost sinners.

"Love so amazing, so divine,
Demands my soul, my life, my all."

2. Glory: the resurrected King! (vv. 22-31)

Verse 21 of Psalm 22 closes the crucifixion of Christ, and verse 22 opens the resurrection section. Verse 22 is quoted in Hebrews 2:11-12, and note that the word "congregation" becomes "church." The emphasis in this last section of Psalm 22 is on *praise* (vv. 22-23, 26), while the emphasis in the first section was on *prayer.*

Before we examine this last section of the psalm, it would be good for us to think about the important relationship between prayer and praise. They certainly go together! In fact, many of the psalms are descriptions of the writer's transition from pain to prayer to praise. Prayer is not simply a means of escape from problems and afflictions. Prayer is an opportunity for God to use our difficulties to glorify His name. When He was ministering on earth, our Lord lived by faith and depended on prayer. The purpose of prayer is the accomplishing of God's will for God's glory. We pray, "Thy will be done" and not "Thy will be changed" if we want to end up praising Him.

Note the various persons who share in this resurrection praise.

A. THE SAVIOUR AND HIS CHURCH (vv. 22, 25). The picture here is that of our Lord singing praises to God in the midst of His brethren, the church. We read of God the Father singing in Zephaniah 3:17, and the Holy Spirit singing in the believer in Ephesians 5:18-20; but here it is the Son of God singing His praises. He had a "song in the night" before He went to the cross (Matt. 26:30), and He had a song after He came forth in victory from the tomb!

At that time, the church was a small body of people; but He saw them as "the great congregation." What joy was in the Saviour's heart when He completed His great work of salvation and came forth in glory and power! He was the last Adam ushering in the new creation (1 Cor. 15:45; 2 Cor. 5:17). He was the Captain of our salvation, leading forth in triumph (Heb. 2:10; 2 Cor. 2:14-16). No longer would He have to contend with bulls, lions, dogs, and wild oxen, for now He was in fellowship with His brethren. (See Matt. 12:46-50; 28:10; as well as John 20:17.)

The phrase "pay my vows" in Psalm 22:25 does not suggest that the Son "made a bargain" with the Father so that the Father would raise Him from the dead. It refers to the Old Testament "peace offering" described in Leviticus 16. As a part of the ceremony, the worshiper invited family and friends to share in a meal at which they ate some of the meat of the sacrifice. Since the Jews did not often get to eat roasted meat, this was a time of joyful feasting. This thought ties in with Psalm 22:26 and 29

B. THE SEED OF ISRAEL (vv. 23-24). Jesus died, not only for the church and to save individuals, but He also died for the people of Israel. "For the transgression of My people was He stricken" (Isa. 53:8). It was necessary that "one Man should die for the people, and that the whole nation perish not" (John 11:50). In His life and death, "Jesus Christ was a minister of the circumcision for the truth of God, to confirm the promises made unto the fathers" (Rom. 15:8). Today, the nation of Israel lives in spiritual blindness (Rom. 11:25ff); but one day they shall see their Messiah, believe, and be saved (Zech. 12:10ff). Then the nation will join in praising the Lord for what He has done for them!

Psalm 22:24 makes it clear that God does not despise or turn away from those who suffer. It may seem that He is deaf and unconcerned, but this is not so. There are higher purposes to suffering than can be seen by unbelieving eyes. The Cross of Jesus Christ is proof of this. The people of Israel have suffered greatly in this world (some of which they brought on themselves), but their suffering has not gone unnoticed by God. He will accomplish His divine purposes on the basis of what Jesus Christ did on Calvary.

C. ALL THE ENDS OF THE EARTH (vv. 26-31). See how the chorus of praise has grown, from the Saviour to the church, then to Israel, and now to the ends of the earth! You find a similar "circle of praise" in Romans 15:8-13. One day, "the earth shall be filled with the knowledge of the glory of the Lord, as the waters cover the sea" (Hab. 2:14).

Who are those who shall share in this anthem of praise? *The meek* and *those who seek God* lead the list. Meekness means submission to God. Notice the sequence of verbs in this section: "Seek Him ... turn unto the Lord ... worship before Thee ... bow before Him ... serve Him" (Ps. 22:26-30). Certainly the world today is not seeking the Lord and bowing before Him! Instead, the world is resisting His truth and rejecting the Saviour. But there will come a day when

"Jesus shall reign, where e'er the sun
Doth His successive journeys run!"

Jesus did not die in vain. One day the announcement will be made: "The kingdoms of this world are become the kingdoms of our Lord, and of His Christ; and He shall reign forever and ever" (Rev. 11:15).

When Satan tempted our Lord in the wilderness, he offered Him all the kingdoms of this world and all their glory, if Jesus would just *once* bow down and worship him. But our Lord knew that there can be no crown without a cross; He first had to suffer and die before He could enter into His glory (Luke 24:25-27). However, Jesus does not have to wait for some future date in order to reign, for even today "the kingdom is the Lord's." He is on His Father's throne today, and all authority in heaven and on earth belongs to Christ (Matt. 28:19-20).

Psalm 22:29 indicates that both rich and poor, high and low, must depend on God for their very life. "The fat upon the earth" are the prosperous people; even they must bow and worship if they would feed on His blessings.

"A seed shall serve Him" (v. 30) means that He shall have a spiritual family because of His death and resurrection. This statement parallels Isaiah 53:10-11. In fact, the writer, with prophetic insight, looked down the centuries and saw that people *yet unborn* would share in the blessings of His righteousness and salvation.

How thrilling it is that the work of Christ on the cross will reach around the world until the end of time! He was crucified in an obscure nation, in the midst of an unimportant people, as far as the world is concerned; and yet that event has eternal consequences for the church, the nation of Israel, and the Gentile nations (see 1 Cor. 10:32). But the important question is: What does Psalm 22 mean to *you* personally? Jesus Christ died on the cross for lost sinners, and that includes all of us. Have you trusted Him? After all, what He purchased on the cross can do you no good until you appropriate it by faith for yourself.

During the administration of President Andrew Jackson, a man named George Wilson was convicted of robbing the

United States mail and was sentenced to be hanged. Intercession was made on Wilson's behalf, and President Jackson granted George Wilson a pardon. *But Wilson refused to accept it!*

The authorities were perplexed, so they turned the problem over to Chief Justice Marshall. This was his conclusion: "A pardon is a slip of paper, the value of which is determined by the acceptance of the person to be pardoned. If it is refused, it is no pardon. George Wilson must be hanged."

Our Lord's death and resurrection have power whether you trust Him or not, but they can have no power *for you* apart from your own personal faith. Will you "eat and be satisfied"? (v. 26) Will you seek Him, turn to Him, and trust Him so that your heart might live?

8
The Song of the Mid-life Crisis

Psalm 71

¹In Thee, O Lord, do I put my trust; let me never be put to confusion. ²Deliver me in Thy righteousness, and cause me to escape; incline Thine ear unto me, and save me. ³Be Thou my strong habitation, whereunto I may continually resort; Thou hast given commandment to save me; for Thou art my rock and my fortress. ⁴Deliver me, O my God, out of the hand of the wicked, out of the hand of the unrighteous and cruel man. ⁵For Thou art my hope, O Lord God, Thou art my trust from my youth. ⁶By Thee have I been holden up from the womb; Thou art He that took me out of my mother's bowels; my praise shall be continually of Thee. ⁷I am as a wonder unto many; but Thou art my strong refuge. ⁸Let my mouth be filled with Thy praise and with Thy honor all the day. ⁹Cast me not off in the time of old age; forsake me not when my strength faileth. ¹⁰For mine enemies speak against me; and they that lay wait for my soul take counsel together, ¹¹Saying, "God hath forsaken him: persecute and take him; for there is none to deliver him." ¹²O God, be not far from me; O my God, make haste for my help. ¹³Let them be confounded and consumed that are adversaries to my soul; let them be covered with reproach and dishonor that seek my hurt. ¹⁴But I will hope continually, and will yet praise Thee more and more. ¹⁵My mouth shall show forth Thy righteousness and Thy salvation all the day; for I know not the numbers thereof. ¹⁶I will go in the strength of the Lord God; I will make mention of Thy righteousness, even of Thine only. ¹⁷*O God, Thou hast taught me from my youth; and hitherto have I declared Thy wondrous works.* ¹⁸*Now also when I am old and grayheaded, O God, forsake me not; until I have showed Thy strength unto this generation, and Thy power to everyone that is to come.* ¹⁹*Thy righteousness also, O God, is very high, who hast done great things; O God, who is like unto Thee?* ²⁰*Thou, which hast showed me great and sore troubles, shalt quicken me again, and shalt bring me up again from the depths of the earth.* ²¹*Thou shalt increase my greatness, and comfort me on every side.* ²²*I will also praise Thee with the psaltery, even Thy truth, O my God; unto Thee will I sing with the harp, O Thou Holy One of Israel.* ²³*My lips shall greatly rejoice when I sing unto Thee; and my soul, which Thou hast redeemed.* ²⁴*My tongue also shall talk of Thy righteousness all the day long; for they are confounded, for they are brought unto shame, that seek my hurt.*

"**I** do hope my Father will let the river of my life go flowing fully until the finish," F.B. Meyer said to a friend. Then the saintly British preacher added, "I don't want it to end in a swamp."

When I read that statement, I recalled hearing the late president of Moody Bible Institute, Dr. William Culbertson, pray, "Lord, help us to end well!"

This psalm was written by a saint who wanted to end well, a man who realized that old age presented its own special dangers and demands even in the life of a believer. He knew that the mature years of life not only created problems, but also *revealed* them—problems that have been hidden in the heart of all during life. The writer had been blessed with a godly childhood and youth (vv. 5-6, 17), so he had an excellent foundation for old age; but he took nothing for granted.

Translators differ in their approach to this psalm. Some translate verses 9 and 18 as though the writer were already in his "declining years." But I feel that this psalm was written by a believer in middle age, contemplating his old age. Verse 18 can be translated, "Even when I am near to old age and being grayheaded." In other words, the psalmist was going through a "mid-life crisis" as he faced his retirement years. Many people have shared this same experience, so any encouragement he can give will certainly be appreciated! The crises of old age do not make us; they show what we are made of already.

You will note that three times in Psalm 71 the writer used the phrase "all the day" (vv. 8, 15, 24). One thing we all have to do, young or old, is learn to live a day at a time, depending on Christ *all* the day. If we try to carry the mistakes of yesterday and the worries about tomorrow, we will only turn today into defeat. "As thy days, so shall thy strength be" (Deut. 33:25).

This phrase "all the day" divides the psalm into three stanzas; and in each of these stanzas, the writer shares a wonderful assurance about God to encourage us in our old age.

1. God will protect us (vv. 1-8)

Whether we like it or not, for most people, the "mature years" are years of growing helplessness. This does not mean that *everybody* suddenly falls apart! We are all "fearfully and wonderfully made," but we are all different. Some of God's "senior saints" are remarkably strong and seem to suffer no physical or mental decline. But, for the most part, each of us slowly begins to discover that the demands are greater than the supplies. A friend told me that he had reached "the metallic age." "I have silver in my hair, gold in my teeth, iron in my vitamin pills, and lead in my shoes!"

As we grow older, we have many fears; and we need a refuge in God. Will we have sufficient funds to pay our bills? Who will take care of us if we have a fall or become ill? Is it safe to live alone? Though some of our "enemies" are imaginary, old age does bring with it some serious problems that cannot be avoided.

But the greatest concern of the writer was that he not be put to shame. He wanted to end well to the glory of God. I heard about one preacher who used to pray, "Lord, deliver me from becoming a mean old man!" A friend said to me, "As I grow into old age, I want to become mellow, not rotten."

The psalmist prayed that God would protect him and be to him a strong habitation, a rock, a fortress. This does not mean that the psalmist wanted to run and hide and escape life. Rather, he needed God as his "refuge and strength" (Ps. 46:1), so that he might be able to face life courageously and glorify God. "I am as a wonder unto many" (v. 7) suggests that others were watching him and marveling at what God did for him. His victories were an encouragement to others as well as a witness to the glory of God.

But the assurance of God's protection is not something that we automatically know and believe. The writer got an early start when it came to putting his trust in God. "By Thee I have been sustained from my birth; Thou art He who took me from my mother's womb" (v. 6, NASB). Like Timothy, the writer was privileged to be born into a home where God was honored and the Word trusted (2 Tim. 1:5).

We do not lay the foundations of our faith in our later years; we must lay them in childhood and youth. For some professing Christians, their "golden years" are really "leaden years" because they wasted their youth and did not lay solid foundations of faith. This does not mean that an older person who has missed his opportunities to live for Christ is automatically a failure. It is never too late to serve God. But the time to start sowing the seed for a "late harvest" of blessing is when we are in our younger years. The psalmist had a real burden to share this truth with the next generation (Ps. 71:18).

Because the psalmist *continually* resorted to the Lord (v. 3), he enjoyed *continual* praise (v. 6). There is a tendency for older people to become critical and bitter and to spend a good deal of time complaining. But this psalm is saturated with praise (vv. 6, 8, 14-16, 22). And this is not occasional and intermittent praise; it is *continual* praise! As we abide in Christ, trust Him, and depend on His grace, we always have something to sing about.

Devotional writer Oswald Chambers told of meeting a man he had known years ago, "a mighty man of God," who had become shallow, talkative, and dead spiritually. In 10 short years, the man had decayed and did not know it. "The fear of sloth and indulgence has come home with a huge fear," Chambers wrote, "and fairly driven me to God to keep me from forgetting what I owe Him." It is good medicine and therapy to praise God. It keeps us young!

As we enter our mature years, we need not fear, because God will protect us. He will be our shelter in the storm, our fortress in the battle. As we continually abide in Him, He will strengthen us and enable us to praise Him; and that praise will keep us from criticizing and complaining. The wicked may accuse, threaten, and attack us, but God will surround and sustain us. He will not always prevent troubles, but He will protect us in troubles and eventually bring us out better than when we went in.

2. God will be with us (vv. 9-15)

Loneliness is a major problem in our "golden years" if we do not know Christ and trust Him. As we grow older, friends and family either move away or die; and sometimes we must relocate, and that means pulling up roots and being transplanted. Sometimes those who ought to care the most pay the least attention to us. Not everybody can afford to live in a busy retirement home where staff experts plan interesting meetings where residents can get to know new people.

The burden of the psalmist's prayer is that God would stay with him during his declining years. "Cast me not off," "Forsake me not," "Be not far from me" (vv. 9, 12). Many older people do feel like "castoffs." It is encouraging to see that some churches provide special ministries for the "golden agers," not only for those who are able to get around, but also for those who are confined. They make sure that their shut-ins get a phone call every day. They provide tapes of the Sunday services for those who cannot attend. In two of the churches I pastored, the young people visited the older members on a regular basis.

It is when we feel lonely and left out that we are most susceptible to the attacks of the enemy. We start to feel sorry for ourselves, and this only makes us critical of others. Self-pity is a terrible weapon in the hands of the adversary.

We do not know who the specific enemies were that the psalmist had to oppose. They were certainly a discouraging crowd, "Saying, God hath forsaken him" (v. 11). They were also selfish, because they wanted him to die so they could get his possessions. We get the impression that they were spreading lies about the psalmist, trying to bring disgrace to his name.

He was too weak to fight them himself (v. 9), so he turned them over to the Lord. He knew that God would be with him no matter what his trials or battles might be. However, one of the problems of old age is *impatience.* The older we grow, the more difficult it is to wait. "Make haste for my help" is his prayer (v. 12). In other words, "Lord, help me—*and do it now!*"

In the previous stanza of this psalm, the writer declared that he would *continually* resort to God (v. 3) and *continually* praise Him (v. 6); and now he adds that he will *continually* hope in the Lord (v. 14). One of my Hebrew lexicons lists seven different words that are translated "hope" in our *King James Version.* The one used in verse 14 means a long and patient waiting in spite of delay and disappointment. It is a hope that is strengthened with bright expectation: we *know* that God is going to meet our needs and accomplish His purposes. The opposite of this "hope" is a feeling of fear and dread.

Keep in mind that "hope" in the Bible is not a self-produced feeling of encouragement that is imaginary, nor is it "wishful thinking" of the "hope-so" variety. A Christian's hope is built on the solid foundation of the character of God and the Word of God. It is this word that Job used when he said of God, "Though He slay me, yet will I trust [hope] in Him" (Job 13:15).

What is a believer's source of hope? It is God! We have hope because God has saved us (Rom. 5:1-2) and certainly He is not going to abandon us (Rom. 8:31-32). We have hope because of the Spirit who lives within us (Rom. 15:13) and because of the Word He has given us (Rom. 15:4). Jesus Christ is our hope (1 Tim. 1:1).

The result of this is "I will . . . yet praise Thee more and more" (v. 14). Here is an optimistic outlook on life! Instead of finding more and more things to complain about, the psalmist found more and more blessings to give praise for!

I mentioned Dr. F.B. Meyer at the beginning of this chapter. One day he met a woman on the train, and he could see that she was depressed and burdened with care. She told him that her crippled daughter had died and this crisis had almost ruined her life. This mother had been accustomed to preparing a meal for her child before leaving for work each morning, and she anticipated the daughter's happy greeting at the end of the day.

Meyer said to her, "When you get home and put the key in the door, say aloud, 'Jesus, I know You are here.' As you light the fire, tell Him what happened during the day. At night, stretch out your hand in the darkness and say, 'Jesus, I know You are here!'"

The same woman met Meyer some weeks later, and he did not recognize her. Instead of lines of misery on her face, there was a smile of joy. "I did as you told me," she said, "and it has made all the difference in my life, and now I feel I know Him."

So far, the two assurances we have discussed center on *our* needs and *our* feelings. If we are not careful, we will become very self-centered! That is why the psalmist added a third assurance

3. God will use us to encourage others (vv. 16-24)

The emphasis in this section is on sharing our personal witness with others, especially those of the next generation (see v. 18). God does not bless us simply that we might enjoy His goodness. He blesses us that we may in turn be a blessing to others. "I will bless thee . . . and thou shalt be a blessing" (Gen. 12:2). It is certainly wonderful to *receive* a blessing, but it is even more wonderful to *be* a blessing!

This truth especially applies to the older saints. Some of them get the idea that, since they have retired from work, they can also retire from ministry. Some of my friends who pastor churches in the large "retirement cities" complain to me that too many able-bodied retirees will not serve the Lord in their local church. "We did our share," they explain. "Now let somebody else do the job."

While it is true that the older officers sometimes need to make room for younger leadership, it is also true that age is no excuse or argument for careless Christian living. "Those that be planted in the house of the Lord shall flourish in the courts of our God. They shall still bring forth fruit in old age" (Ps. 92:13-14).

To begin with, we need to minister *in our daily walk*. "I will go in the strength of the Lord God" (Ps. 71:16a). We have no strength of our own; our power for living must come from Christ. "I can do all things through Christ which strengtheneth me" (Phil. 4:13). The psalmist wanted to show God's strength to the next generation (v. 18) that the younger believers might learn to trust God.

Blessed is that church that has a group of senior saints whose walk honors the Lord. Age is no guarantee of maturity or wisdom. There are old fools as well as young fools! But when the "elders of the land" glorify God in their lives, this is a tremendous encouragement to any church. Paul encouraged Titus to show respect to godly "senior saints" and to let them help teach the younger ones in the church (Titus 2:1-5).

Older Christians should glorify God in their walk and also in their *words.* "I will make mention of Thy righteousness" (v. 16). Mature believers who have been through the difficult experiences of life can teach younger believers a great deal about the Christian life. Personally, I thank God for the older believers who have helped me in my life and ministry, men and women who could pray, encourage, rebuke in love, and teach me more about God. Just watching their lives was a great encouragement!

Notice the emphasis on the righteousness of God (vv. 16, 19, 24). The longer we walk with God, the clearer we see His ways and understand His heart. A younger Christian is prone to question God and wonder if the Father really is doing the right thing. But a mature saint knows that the Judge of all the earth will do right (Gen. 18:25). There are no mistakes in His plans.

We encourage others by our walk and our witness. We also encourage others by *the way we go through testing.* I like the way *The New Berkley Version* translates Psalm 71:20-21: "Thou, who has made me experience troubles great and sore, wilt revive me again and wilt bring me up again from the depths of the earth. Thou wilt add to my stature, and comfort me again."

In spite of their knowledge and experience, the senior saints have their days of testing and discouragement. Abraham faced his greatest test when he was well over 100 years of age! No matter how old we are, there are still new lessons to learn and new territory to conquer. We must never stop growing in spiritual stature.

These verses assure us that God is in control of all testing, and that He will revive us when we feel dead, resurrect us when we feel low, and renew and enlarge us in our spiritual life. Job was not a young man when he experienced that great affliction, and just think of how he has encouraged suffering saints down through the centuries!

For most of us, getting older creates new problems and makes new demands on us. Yet each challenge is an opportunity for spiritual growth for ourselves and encouragement for others. Through our lives, younger believers can see the strength and power of the Lord.

The psalm ends on a high note of praise and song. The psalmist used his hands to praise God, for he played the harp. He used his lips to praise God as he sang joyfully of his redemption. All the day he was sharing with others what God had done for him. That certainly is better than sitting around and complaining!

Whatever happened to the enemies that he was so worried about?

He was concerned in verse 1 that he not be put to shame by failing the Lord, and thus give grounds to the enemy to attack. He prayed in verse 13 that the enemy might be confounded, and the answer to that prayer is recorded in verse 24: "For they [the enemy] are confounded, for they are brought unto shame, that seek my hurt."

The lesson is clear: occupy yourself with the Lord, and He will take care of your enemies. Fill your day with praise to the Lord and that praise will defeat your foes. Along with your praise, pray to Him for help; and be sure to give witness to those around you. This is a combination that is unbeatable!

You may not be going through a mid-life crisis, or even be in your retirement years. Perhaps you are a younger person. So much the better! *Start now* to make your "golden years" happy years. What you are going to be *then* you are becoming right now. The seed you are sowing now will give the harvest in later years. We know not how long we will live, or when the Lord will return; so we must prepare for the future. The best way to meet the Lord is by faithfully doing His will each day. Then you will always be ready!

It has well been said that the important thing is not so much that we add years to our life as life to our years. What shall it profit a man if he shall live a long life and be miserable, and make other people miserable!

Determine now, by the grace of God, to "end well." Don't allow the river of your life to end in a swamp.

9
Listen! God Is Laughing!

Psalm 2

¹Why do the heathen rage, and the people imagine a vain thing? ²The kings of the earth set themselves, and the rulers take counsel together, against the Lord, and against His Anointed, saying, ³"Let us break their bands asunder, and cast away their cords from us." ⁴He that sitteth in the heavens shall laugh, the Lord shall have them in derision. ⁵Then shall He speak unto them in His wrath, and vex them in His sore displeasure. ⁶"Yet have I set My King upon My holy hill of Zion. ⁷I will declare the decree: the Lord hath said unto Me, 'Thou art My Son; this day have I begotten Thee. ⁸Ask of Me and I shall give Thee the heathen for Thine inheritance, and the uttermost parts of the earth for Thy possession. ⁹Thou shalt break them with a rod of iron; Thou shalt dash them in pieces like a potter's vessel.'" ¹⁰Be wise now therefore, O ye kings; be instructed, ye judges of the earth. ¹¹Serve the Lord with fear, and rejoice with trembling. ¹²Kiss the Son, lest He be angry, and ye perish from the way, when His wrath His kindled but a little. Blessed are all they that put their trust in Him.

A restaurant in Michigan offers three minutes of silence on the jukebox at the same price as a regular recording.

A high-rise resident in Chicago threatened to sue a nearby church if members continued to ring the church bell on Sunday mornings when he wanted to sleep.

Doctors have discovered hearing damage in teens who are exposed to a great deal of rock music.

What does it add up to? One of the most serious problems of modern life: noise pollution. We are surrounded by noise that we don't even hear because we are so accustomed to it! Yet that noise is doing damage whether we recognize it or not.

Added to the increase in noise is the increase in the number of voices that cry for our attention. Advertisers, promoters, preachers, politicians, entertainers are calling to us (sometimes shouting at us), begging for our attention and obedience.

How can we make sense out of all the noise in our world today? Psalm 2 helps us solve this important problem. The Psalmist David (Acts 4:25) invites us to hear four voices and understand what they are saying.

1. The voice of the nations—defiance (Ps. 2:1-3)

What an amazing thing: the nations of the world united to defy God and cast off His authority! If the nations only realized how good God has been to them, they would bow down in glad submission. After all, it is God who provides for the nations. Paul reminded the people of Lystra that God "did good, and gave us rain from heaven, and fruitful seasons, filling our hearts with food and gladness" (Acts 14:17). God has also "determined the times before appointed, and the bounds of their habitation" (Acts 17:26). Even more important, God sent His Son to be the Saviour of the world. What more could He do?

Instead of rejoicing in God's blessing, the nations of the earth are rebelling against God's rule over them. They want to be free! The picture here is of a stubborn, rebellious animal that wants to break the yoke. "We will not have this Man to reign over us" (Luke 19:14). Their rebellion is not simply against the Lord, as some "abstract being," but also "against His anointed [Christ]."

From the beginning of human history, man has rebelled against God in a selfish desire for freedom. Our first parents wanted freedom and, in their disobedience, inherited slavery. The great cry of the nations today is for national freedom and self-government and independence. Many new nations act like adolescents with their newfound freedom. But even apart from the surface political problems is the deeper spiritual problem of rebellion against God. Instead of submitting to God's moral and spiritual laws, the nations are "doing their own thing" and resisting God's will.

The description of this spiritual rebellion is found in Romans 1:18ff. Man knew the truth but preferred to believe a lie: "For they exchanged the truth of God for a lie, and worshiped and served the creature rather than the Creator" (Rom. 1:25, NASB). Man thus became his own god! Satan got what he wanted: "You will be like God" (Gen. 3:5, NASB).

In the rejection of Jesus Christ and in the persecution of the church, this rebellion reached a climax (Acts 4:23-30). It will reach another climax at the end of the age when the nations assemble at Armageddon to fight Jesus Christ (Zech. 12:1-9; 14:1-4; Matt. 24:27-30; Rev. 19:17-21). During this age, this united rebellion reveals itself in man's refusal to obey God's laws, and in his attempts to change the consequences.

But God calls this effort "a vain thing" (v. 1). Why? Because God knows that *it is impossible to have true freedom apart from submission to authority.* If there were no laws in your city, for example, you would not be free to drive safely on the streets, go shopping, build a house, or borrow a book at the library. True freedom is based on law, and God is the law-giver.

Freedom without authority is anarchy. Authority without freedom is slavery. True freedom is liberty under authority. It is a vain thing to think that man can be free without God. The history of man is the record of new "freedoms" that led only to new slavery. Every step man has taken to break free from God's moral law has only brought him into more bondage. Why? Because man is made in the image of God; so, when he rebels against God, *he is really rebelling against himself!*

In one of his books, the theologian P.T. Forsyth wrote, "The purpose of life is not to find your freedom, but to find your master." This is true in every area of life. The athlete cannot find his freedom of expression to use his skills unless he learns to submit to his coach. The student must submit to the teacher, the apprentice to the master craftsman. True freedom is found, not in doing whatever you want to do, but in being all that God wills for you. "I delight to do Thy will, O my God: yea, Thy Law is within my heart" (Ps. 40:8). That is freedom.

2. The voice of the Father—derision (Ps. 2:4-6)

What a contrast between the scene on earth and the situation in heaven! The nations of the earth are in tumult,   raging like beasts; but God is on His throne in heaven, calmly watching. Men are boldly shaking their fists against heaven— and God is laughing! Almighty God ridicules the attacks of puny men. "The Lord shall laugh at him: for He seeth that his day is coming" (Ps. 37:13).   "But Thou, O Lord, dost laugh at them; Thou dost scoff at all the nations" (Ps. 59:8, NASB). "Behold, the nations are as a drop of a bucket,   and are counted as the small dust of the balance"   (Isa. 40:15).

God maintains His authority whether men accept it or not. God is still the supreme Ruler of the universe; His laws are still in force; and His judgments are certain. If man cooperates with the laws of God, he will succeed. If he resists those laws, he will fail and be destroyed. God is speaking today in nature, in His Word, and in the human conscience; yet man will not listen. God is speaking today in grace, but one day He will begin to speak in judgment.

Verse 5 of Psalm 2 states that one day God will speak in

His wrath. He is speaking today in His wrath, according to Romans 1:18. In what way? *By allowing man to have his own way and suffer the consequences!* Three times in Romans 1 it states that "God gave them up" (vv. 24, 26, 28). He let them have their own way! He did not interfere with their decisions or with the consequences. He permitted His moral law to work out its full effect. The result? Mankind exchanged truth for lies, God's glory for idols, spirituality for sensuality, and life for death. The greatest judgment God can send to a person is not fire from heaven, but simply letting that person do what he wants to do and suffer the consequences.

However, there is coming a day of wrath when God shall "speak unto them in His wrath, and vex them in His sore displeasure" (v. 5). Since Calvary, God has not been sending His judgments on the earth; but in time, the day of judgment will dawn. In the Bible this period is called "the Tribulation" or "Great Tribulation" (Rev. 6—19 describes this period). Jesus said, "For then shall be great tribulation, such as was not since the beginning of the world to this time, no, nor ever shall be" (Matt. 24:21).

This psalm undoubtedly had its origin in some personal experience of David when he was made King of Israel. Perhaps some of the surrounding nations resisted his authority, and God enabled him to bring them to submission. But Acts 4:23-30 gives us the authority to interpret Psalm 2 in the light of the Person and work of Jesus Christ. *He* is the King; He is enthroned in the heavenly Zion today (see Heb. 12:22ff). One day He shall return and sit on the throne of David (Luke 1:32-33); but meanwhile, "He must reign, till He hath put all enemies under His feet" (1 Cor. 15:25).

According to the Epistle of Hebrews, Jesus Christ serves in heaven today as a high priest "after the order of Melchizedek" (Heb. 5:9-10). Melchizedek was both king and priest (Heb. 7:1-3; Gen. 14:17-24). In the Old Testament, there were prophets who were also priests (Jeremiah, for example), and kings who were prophets (David is an example); but

Melchizedek is the only historic person who was both priest and king. When King Uzziah tried to invade the priesthood, God judged him (2 Chron. 26:16ff).

"Melchizedek" means "king of righteousness." He was King of Salem, which means "peace." It is only when Jesus Christ is permitted to reign that we can have both righteousness and peace. In our world today, we have sin and war, because the nations have rejected God's King.

There will be no peace on earth until Jesus Christ reigns from David's throne. Until then, we will have the same situation that existed during the period of the Judges: "In those days there was no king in Israel, but every man did that which was right in his own eyes" (Jud. 17:6; and see 18:1; 19:1; also 21:25).

Whether men like it or not, God has made Jesus Christ "the Ruler of the kings of the earth" (Rev. 1:5, NASB). No wonder the Father laughs as He sees the kings of the earth rebel!

3. The voice of the Son—declaration (Ps. 2:7-9)

God the Son now speaks and declares that man's devices cannot change God's decrees. God gives man freedom even to rebel, but man's rebellion can never thwart God's eternal purposes. Even when the Jews and Gentiles united to crucify Christ, they unconsciously fulfilled "the determinate counsel and foreknowledge of God" (Acts 2:23). The early church interpreted Psalm 2 in this way (Acts 4:23-28, and note especially verse 28).

The declaration in these verses reveals several important truths. First of all, Jesus Christ is God: "Thou art My Son." There are echoes of this statement at our Lord's baptism (Matt. 3:17) and Transfiguration (Matt. 17:5). If Jesus were only a "good man" or a "godly teacher," He could never be sharing the throne of God in heaven! This was the argument Peter presented at Pentecost (see Acts 2:29-36, and also Heb. 1:5; 5:5).

Second, our Lord's enthronement was a very special

event: "This day have I begotten Thee" (Ps. 2:7). This is not a reference to His birth at Bethlehem, for that was an event clothed with weakness and humility. According to Acts 13:33, this is a reference to our Lord's resurrection. The "virgin tomb," as it were, gave birth to the glorified Son of God! Jesus Christ was "begotten" into a whole new kind of life at His resurrection and ascension, for in Him *glorified humanity permanently entered heaven.*

Of course, His resurrection and enthronement go together. He was "declared to be the Son of God with power . . . by the resurrection from the dead" (Rom. 1:4). As the Son of God, He rightfully deserves to be on the throne. "The Lord [God the Father] said unto my Lord [God the Son], 'Sit Thou at My right hand, until I make Thine enemies Thy footstool'" (Ps. 110:1, and see Matt. 21:41-46). God had decreed this from all eternity, and the sinful rebellion of man could never hinder it from being fulfilled.

Jesus Christ is not only the Son of God and the reigning King, but He is also the Judge (Psalm 2:8-9). One day He shall return and smash the nations into pieces the way a potter smashes useless pottery (see Dan. 2:44; Matt. 21:43-44; Rev. 12:5; 19:15). Men think *they* are ruling, but men are only clay vessels, weak, and easily shattered.

The nations that are rebelling against Christ today will one day be a part of His kingdom inheritance. Satan offered Christ "all the kingdoms of the world, and the glory of them" (Matt. 4:8), if Christ would worship him only once; but Jesus will not accept His inheritance from the devil. "Ask of Me," said the Father; and one day Jesus will ask and enter into His glorious kingdom (Rev. 11:15). Satan offered Him a "shortcut," but Jesus Christ purchased His inheritance by His sacrificial death on the cross.

Those who submit to Christ will one day share in His victory and His kingdom (Rev. 2:26-27). Those who rebel will be cast into outer darkness forever (2 Thes. 1:7-10; Luke 19:27).

It may seem that man is having his way in this world, but

God's decrees still stand: "I have spoken it, I will also bring it to pass; I have purposed it, I will also do it" (Isa. 46:11). He will fulfill His purposes, and the proof of it is the fact that He raised Jesus Christ from the dead and enthroned Him in heaven!

4. The voice of the Holy Spirit—decision (Ps. 2:10-12)

These closing verses are an appeal from God for men to stop rebelling.

First, He appeals to *the mind* (v. 10). "Be wise...be instructed." In other words, "Get smart!" What man is doing appears to be logical and reasonable, but it is only evidence of man's ignorance. "Professing themselves to be wise, they became fools" (Rom. 1:22). Man has no fear of God; therefore, he has no wisdom, for "the fear of the Lord is the beginning of wisdom" (Ps. 111:10).

One of our great problems today is the fact that man has a great deal of knowledge but very little wisdom. Wisdom is the ability to use knowledge for the best purposes. We have unlocked the power of the atom, but now we don't know how to control it. We are, like Dr. Frankenstein, the victims of the monsters we create. Every "breakthrough" in science usually means the "breakup" of something else. Our insecticides kill the pests, but they also upset the balance of nature and help create ecological problems far more serious than the pests. Knowledge without wisdom makes man both a tyrant and a victim.

While we as Christians appreciate the insights of "the humanities," and thank God for education, we also recognize the danger of *humanism*—the religion that puts man in the center and leaves God out completely. Satan's offer in the Garden of Eden was *knowledge without God,* and today we see the sad consequences.

The Holy Spirit's second appeal is to *the will:* "Serve the Lord with fear" (Ps. 2:11). Note that the result will be *joy,* not the joy of "doing your own thing," but the joy of fulfilling God's will in submission to Him. *Everyone is serving something.* Nobody is free, and those people who think they are free are in the greatest bondage. Some people are serving their bodies (Rom. 6:12-13) and the various appetites of the flesh (Titus 3:3).

Rebellion is caused by pride, and pride is a sin of the will. It was pride that transformed Lucifer into Satan (Isa. 14:12-14). Nations are proud of their territory and resources, and forget that all of these blessings are given to them by God so that they might serve Him (Acts 17:26-28). Now these blessings are causing national and international problems because God has been left out.

The Spirit's third appeal is to *the heart:* In Psalm 2:12, "kiss the Son" is a reference to the ancient practice of showing homage to the new monarch by kissing his hand or even his foot. The immediate reference in the psalm was to the coronation of David, at which the various rulers paid homage and pledged their service. But the larger meaning is to Jesus Christ, the Son of David.

Suppose that men do not submit to Him? Then what? *They will perish when He reveals His anger!* Today, Jesus Christ is God's Lamb (John 1:29); but one day, the Lamb will become the Lion (Rev. 5:5-6) and will pour out His wrath on the rebels of the earth.

Years ago, I heard a story in an evangelist's sermon that I cannot forget, even though I have forgotten the sermon. In a frontier town, a horse bolted and ran away with a wagon that had a little child in it. Seeing that the child was in danger, a young man risked his life to catch the horse and stop it.

The child who was saved grew up to become a lawless man, and one day he stood before a judge to be sentenced for a serious crime. The prisoner recognized the judge as the man who, years before, had saved his life; so he pled for mercy on the basis of that experience. But the words from the bench silenced all of his pleas:

"Young man, *then* I was your saviour; *today* I am your

judge, and I must sentence you to be hanged."

One day Jesus Christ will say to rebellious sinners, "During that long day of grace, I was the Saviour, and I would have forgiven you. But today I am your Judge. Depart from Me, ye cursed, into everlasting fire!"

"Kiss the Son!" After all, He kissed you when He died for you on the cross. It was at Calvary that mercy and truth met together, and righteousness and peace kissed each other (Ps. 85:10). It is only at Calvary that you can find righteousness and peace, by trusting Him who is the King of righteousness and the King of peace!

Today, God is speaking in grace. Tomorrow, He will speak in wrath

10

The Singing Soldier

Psalm 27

¹The Lord is my light and my salvation; whom shall I fear? The Lord is the strength of my life; of whom shall I be afraid? ²When the wicked, even mine enemies and my foes, came upon me to eat up my flesh, they stumbled and fell. ³Though a host should encamp against me, my heart shall not fear; though war should rise against me, in this will I be confident. ⁴One thing have I desired of the Lord, that will I seek after; that I may dwell in the house of the Lord all the days of my life, to behold the beauty of the Lord, and to inquire in His temple. ⁵For in the time of trouble He shall hide me in His pavilion; in the secret of His tabernacle shall He hide me; He shall set me up upon a rock. ⁶And now shall mine head be lifted up above mine enemies round about me; therefore will I offer in His tabernacle sacrifices of joy; I will sing, yea, I will sing praises unto the Lord. ⁷Hear, O Lord, when I cry with my voice, have mercy also upon me, and answer me. ⁸When Thou saidst, "Seek ye My face," my heart said unto Thee, "Thy face, Lord, will I seek." ⁹Hide not Thy face far from me; put not Thy servant away in anger; Thou hast been my help; leave me not, neither forsake me, O God of my salvation. ¹⁰When my father and my mother forsake me, then the Lord will take me up. ¹¹Teach me Thy way, O Lord, and lead me in a plain path, because of mine enemies. ¹²Deliver me not over unto the will of mine enemies; for false witnesses are risen up against me, and such as breathe out cruelty. ¹³I had fainted, unless

*I had believed to see the goodness of the Lord in the land of the
living. 14Wait on the Lord, be of good courage, and He shall
strengthen thine heart. Wait, I say, on the Lord.*

It was March 4, 1933. The United States was in the terrifying
clutches of economic depression. The newly elected president, Franklin Delano Roosevelt, believed that the greatest
problem was not the absence of finances but the presence of
fear. In his inaugural address, he spoke one sentence that has
been often quoted: "The only thing we have to fear is fear
itself."

Henry David Thoreau wrote similar words in his journal
entry of September 7, 1851: "Nothing is so much to be feared
as fear." Perhaps he got the idea from Francis Bacon (1561-
1626) who wrote, "Nothing is terrible except fear itself." And
the Duke of Wellington is supposed to have said, "The only
thing I am afraid of is fear."

These quotations bear witness to the fact that fear is a real
problem in every age and in the heart of every people.
Doctors tell us that fear performs a good physical function
because it triggers certain glands in the body that, in turn,
release substances that enable us to do amazing things. But
when fear grips the heart, the body is paralyzed.

Whether David wrote this psalm during the time King Saul
was hounding him, or when his own son Absalom turned
against him, we do not know. But we do know that David was
facing enemies (vv. 2, 6, 11-12) and was tempted to be afraid
(vv. 1, 3). But he did not give in to his fears; and in this psalm
we can trace his experiences and discover how we can have
victory over fear.

1. Warring (vv. 1-3)
God's people have enemies. The nation of Israel was often
attacked by enemies; the prophets aroused the opposition of
unbelievers; even the early church experienced attack

from religious people. Our Lord came with a message of peace, but sometimes the result is war (Matt. 10:32-39). The believer who somehow avoids persecution is either hiding his light or compromising the truth. It is impossible to escape opposition once you have made your stand for Christ.

We must keep in mind that our enemies (the flesh and blood variety) are tools of the *real* enemy, Satan. "For our struggle is not against flesh and blood, but against the rulers, against the powers, against the world forces of this darkness, against the spiritual forces of wickedness in the heavenly places" (Eph. 6:12, NASB). Knowing that the people who oppose us are only being used by the devil enables us to love them and pray for them as Jesus commanded us to do (Matt. 5:43-48).

Sometimes an enemy suddenly comes upon us (Ps. 27:2); and at other times, the enemy sets up camp and begins a long siege (v. 3). David saw his foes as wild beasts, stalking him in order to eat him up. Their very breath was cruelty (v. 12, and see Acts 9:1). But he was not afraid, for his confidence was in God.

"In this will I be confident" he cried. In what? In God, who was his light, salvation, and strength! (Ps. 27:1)

Light is a significant symbol of God. God is compared to the sun (Ps. 84:11), which is the source of life for our world. Enemies like to attack at night and catch us off guard, but if we are "walking in the light," they will only fail (1 John 1:5-7). "Do not gloat over me, my enemy! Though I have fallen, I will rise. Though I sit in darkness, the Lord will be my light" (Micah 7:8, NIV).

Because God is our light, He is our salvation. David called Him the "God of my salvation" (Ps. 27:9). The Hebrew word translated "salvation" is the name "Joshua"—Jehovah is salvation; and the Greek version is "Jesus." In the Old Testament, "salvation" usually refers to deliverance from physical danger; but the spiritual meaning is not lacking (Pss. 51:14; 79:9).

When the enemy attacks us, God is also our strength, or stronghold. The word describes a fortress into which the enemy cannot penetrate. The same image is found in Psalm 46:1: "God is our refuge and strength." Since David was an outdoorsman, he often used images from nature to describe God; the "rock" or "fortress" is one of the most frequent. (See Ps. 18:1-2, for example.)

But this word also describes strength that God gives to His people in times of attack. We do not run into the fortress to hide but to get the power needed to go back and face the enemy. God is our fortress around us and our force within us, and with His help we defeat the enemy. To a New Testament believer, this is the power of the Spirit of God who enables us to be good soldiers of Jesus Christ (Eph. 6:10ff; 3:20-21).

No matter what kind of experience or equipment a soldier might have, if he has fear in his heart, he will fail. "My heart shall not fear" affirmed David (Ps. 27:3). Fear in the heart always makes the enemy look bigger and tempts us to walk by sight and not by faith. "Why are ye so fearful? How is it that ye have no faith?" (Mark 4:40)

What was the secret of David's fearless confidence in battle? The second experience described in the psalm gives us the answer.

2. Worshiping (Ps. 27:4-6)

One rainy day, my wife and I visited the famous battlefield of Waterloo in Belgium where Wellington defeated Napoleon. Except for the souvenirs in the shops, and the movie that attempts to recreate the battle, you would never know that a war had been won there. As I looked at the huge mound with the monument on the top (I was too weary to climb the hill!), I remembered what Wellington was supposed to have said: "The Battle of Waterloo was won on the playing fields of Eton."

In David's case, the battles were won *in his private times of worship with the Lord.* David had many responsibilities, and there were many demands upon his time; but his number one priority was seeking God's face. He said, like Paul, "This one thing I do" (Phil. 3:13). Instead of being like Paul and David, God's people are too often like Martha who did not make time to fellowship with Christ. We need to hear Jesus say, "One thing is needful" (Luke 10:42).

Without satisfying worship, there can be no successful warfare. How did David know that God was a light, a deliverer, and a fortress? He learned it while gazing on God's glory in his time of worship and meditation. David envied the priests who were privileged to dwell close to God's house and even enter the courts and the holy place. (Perhaps the priests envied David for his exploits and travels!) How David longed to leave the battlefield and dwell in God's house! But, wherever he was, he took time to come into God's presence, meditate on God's gracious kindness ("beauty" in Ps. 27:4), and contemplate ("enquire") the person of God.

In David's day, the temple was not yet built; and the ark of God was kept in a tent. (The word "temple" in v. 4 simply means "palace, sanctuary." It was used for God's sanctuary though the structure was a tent. See 1 Sam. 1:9; 3:3.) But this image of a tent conveys a beautiful spiritual truth in Ps. 27:5. In Eastern countries, when you are invited into a Bedouin's tent to eat and rest, you are automatically protected by your host. You are safer in the tent than if you were hiding in a cave, for all of the sheik's resources would be at your disposal!

When David came into God's presence in worship, it was like entering the tent of the sheik: God welcomed David and protected him. Because he was not a priest, David could not go into the tabernacle, but he could enjoy the same spiritual experience. This is the imagery behind Psalm 91. The phrase "under His wings" (91:4) probably refers to the wings of the cherubim in the holy of holies (Ex. 25:17-22).

God's people today have the privilege of entering into

God's presence through the merits of Jesus Christ (Heb. 10:19ff). In fact, we can *live* in the holy of holies! The privilege that David longed for is ours today, and yet we fail to take advantage of it. This explains why we so often are defeated in the battles of life, for if we would be successful warriors, we must first be successful worshipers. If we ignore His presence, we forfeit His protection.

Psalm 27:6 states a basic truth: when we lift up our eyes to behold the Lord, He will lift up our head above our enemies. A bowed head, of course, is a sign of defeat. "But Thou, O Lord, art a shield for me; my glory, and the lifter up of mine head" (Ps. 3:3). Those who trust the Lord can lift their heads high, not in pride, but in victory to the glory of God.

In his worship, David not only sought the Lord and gazed upon His glory, but he also praised Him in song. He brought the "sacrifice of praise" to the Lord (Heb. 13:15), a privilege we have as the priests of God (1 Peter 2:5). How easy it is to plead with the Lord in the midst of the battle and then forget to praise Him after He has given us the victory.

Worship is one of the great needs in personal lives, and in churches, today. The victories on the battlefield are won in the prayer closet. "Praying always with all prayer and supplication in the Spirit" (Eph. 6:18) is as much a part of spiritual victory as putting on the armor and using the sword.

3. Walking (Ps. 27:7-12)

The "atmosphere" of the psalm changes at this point, for we move out of the tabernacle and into the marketplace and the daily demands of life. We cannot stay on the mountaintop and behold God's glory; we must descend into the valley and share the glory with others (Matt. 17:1-21). Often it is in the "daily round" that we face our greatest temptations and meet our greatest defeats.

David's great concern is that God will not forsake him but will walk with him and deliver him. It is one thing to

see God's beauty in the house of worship and something else
to practice His presence on the path of life. The answer is to
keep seeking God's face no matter where we may be. It is
God who invites us to seek Him, and we should *immediately*
respond by turning to Him in love and worship.

Psalm 27:8 states an important spiritual truth: be sensitive
to God's voice and, when He speaks, immediately respond to
Him. You may be driving your car, pushing a shopping cart, or
mowing the lawn, but if God touches your heart, pause to
worship Him and to seek His face. You need not stop what
you are doing, although it is good to do so when you can.
Simply lift your heart in loving praise to Him! These little
"blessing breaks" during the day will help keep you fresh and
encouraged in the Lord, and they will help make you a
blessing to others.

No believer today need pray verse 9, because God has
promised, "I will never leave thee, nor forsake thee" (Heb.
13:5). The *fact* of God's presence with us is assured by His
promise, but the *experience* of His presence depends on how
we relate to Him in faith, love, obedience, and desire. There
is a difference in the Christian life between "union" (belong-
ing to Christ) and "communion" (enjoying fellowship with
Christ).

A father and a mother might possibly forsake a child, but it
is not likely. However, God is to us a devoted and faithful
Father (Ps. 103:13), but He also tenderly deals with us as
would a loving mother (Isa. 49:15). As children in God's
family, we have a Saviour who is closer than a brother, and a
Father who is both father and mother to us in all the
demands of life.

As we walk the path of life, we need direction and guidance, and this is the burden of the prayer in verses 11-12.
"Teach me . . . lead me. . . . Deliver me." The enemy is
always present to trip us up and to get us on attractive
detours. No matter what the contour of the land might be,
God wants to lead us on a "level [plain] path" so that we will
not trip and fall. Satan wants to lead us on crooked

paths that are uneven and treacherous.

Our motive for wanting to know and do God's will is that He might be glorified: "He leadeth me in the paths of righteousness for His name's sake" (Ps. 23:3). The enemy is watching! The false witnesses would like to become *true* witnesses and find something to accuse in our lives. When David committed his great sin with Bathsheba, it gave "great occasion to the enemies of the Lord to blaspheme" (2 Sam. 12:14). More damage is done to the work of God by good people doing bad things than by bad people doing bad things. The bad example of a good person is a terrible weapon in the hands of Satan.

The secret is in the heart. "My heart shall not fear" (Ps. 27:3) because "my heart said unto Thee, 'Thy face, Lord, will I seek'" (v. 8). When we seek the face of God, we cannot fear! As long as we look to Him by faith, He will guide us on the right path; and we will not give the enemy occasion to slander His name.

We have shared three experiences with David: warring, worshiping, and walking. But the fourth experience is the most difficult, and yet it is important to us if we are going to overcome fear.

4. Waiting (vv. 13-14)

I must confess that it is easier for me to *write* about waiting than it is to *practice* it! By nature, I am an activist, and I don't like to be kept waiting! The Lord knows this, so He constantly arranges for me to get into the slowest line at the airport, the stalled lane on the highway, and the crowded restaurant at lunchtime. One of these days, He hopes I will learn better how to wait!

Just as the pauses in music help make it more beautiful, so the "waiting periods" of life add beauty and grace to our characters. There are times when God calls on us to act, and we must not delay. But there are also times when God calls upon us to wait *so that He may act,* and we dare not interfere. It has well been said that God's delays are not

God's denials; they are only preparation for greater blessing.

David had prayed for God's will in verse 11, but the will of God involves *the right time* as well as the right actions and motives. To do a right thing at the wrong time is to disobey the will of God. When God says, "Wait!" it is because there is yet work for Him to do, either *in* us or *for* us, to prepare us for His blessing.

Again, the secret of waiting is in the heart. *It takes as much courage to wait as it does to war.* The successful general plans his strategy and knows exactly when to attack. As we wait before the Lord in worship, and walk with Him daily, He puts strength into our hearts. Faith is evidenced as much in patience as in performance (Heb. 6:12; 10:36). The *waiters* need faith just as do the warriors.

Verse 13 makes it clear that it is *faith* that sees us through. "I had fainted, unless I had believed to see." The world says, "Seeing is believing," but for a Christian, believing is seeing. Like Elisha's servant, we need to have our eyes opened to see how mighty God's army is (2 Kings 6:15-17).

When we win spiritual battles, we promote "the goodness of the Lord" (Ps. 27:13). In human history, men have fought wars because of evil motives and desires; but the Christian warfare is constructive, not destructive. We tear down that we might build up, and we uproot that we might plant better seed (Jer. 1:10). The two-edged sword of the Word of God slays in order that it might make alive (Heb. 4:12).

The opposite of courage is fainting, and the thing that keeps us from fainting is faith in God. "Men ought always to pray, and not to faint" (Luke 18:1). In the Christian life, waiting is not inactivity, doing nothing. Waiting is preparation for the next battle, the next blessing. As we wait, we pray; we meditate on the Word; we worship God. The wise sailor repairs his sails in calm weather, and the wise soldier regathers his strength during the lull in the battle. "They that wait upon the Lord shall renew [exchange] their strength" (Isa. 40:31).

The ability to calm your soul and wait before God is one of the most difficult things in the Christian life. Our old nature is restless. The world around us is frantically in a hurry. Even some of our Christian friends might suggest that we are "backslidden" because we are not running to every seminar, listening to every visiting speaker, and attending every religious meeting. Years ago, Dr. A.W. Tozer suggested that the church might experience revival if we would cancel all of our meetings and just gather for prayer and worship!

God can help us conquer fear if we will learn to worship, walk, and wait; and the most difficult of these is—*wait.* A restless heart usually leads to a reckless life. All religious activity is not necessarily ministry. Instead of building us up, it might be tearing us down.

"My soul, wait thou only upon God; for my expectation is from Him. He only is my rock and my salvation; He is my defense; I shall not be moved" (Ps. 62:5-6).

11
Life's Second Most Important Question

Psalm 8

¹O Lord our Lord, how excellent is Thy name in all the earth! Who hast set Thy glory above the heavens. ²Out of the mouth of babes and sucklings hast Thou ordained strength because of Thine enemies, that Thou mightest still the enemy and the avenger. ³When I consider Thy heavens, the work of Thy fingers, the moon and the stars, which Thou hast ordained; ⁴What is man, that Thou art mindful of him? And the son of man, that Thou visitest him? ⁵For Thou hast made him a little lower than the angels, and hast crowned him with glory and honor. ⁶Thou madest him to have dominion over the works of Thy hands; Thou hast put all things under his feet, ⁷All sheep and oxen, yea, and the beasts of the field; ⁸The fowl of the air, and the fish of the sea, and whatsoever passeth through the paths of the seas. ⁹O Lord our Lord, how excellent is Thy name in all the earth!

"What think ye of Christ?" (Matt. 22:42) is probably life's most important question, for a wrong answer means eternal condemnation. "Unless you believe that I am He, you shall die in your sins" (John 8:24, NASB).

But Psalm 8:4 poses life's *second* most important question: "What is man?" Is man only a highly developed animal, as Darwin taught, or an underdeveloped child, as Freud believed? Or perhaps man is only an economic factor, as Karl Marx believed. It is interesting that Luke 15 presents all three pictures: the animal—a lost sheep; the economic factor—a lost coin; the spoiled child—the prodigal son!

Plato once defined man as "a featherless biped." One of his rivals showed up with a plucked chicken and announced, "Behold, Plato's man!" Perhaps that was when Plato changed his definition to "a being in search of meaning." Pascal said man was "a reed, but a thinking reed." Mark Twain apologized for man by explaining that God made man at the end of the week when Deity was tired!

What man thinks of man may be important, but most important is what God thinks of man. In Psalm 8, David had the courage to declare that man was—a king! God crowned him with glory and honor! Then, why isn't man *acting* like a king? Why is he in so much trouble when God gave him authority and dominion? The history of mankind shows that man behaves more like a slave than a sovereign! There must be something wrong.

There *is* something wrong, and Psalm 8 explains what it is. In order to understand man's place in the universe, and in order to fulfill it, we need to meet the three "kings" who are involved in this psalm.

1. King Adam

We must go back to Creation if we are to understand who man is and what man is supposed to do. The record is given in Genesis 1:26-28, verses that are quoted in Psalm 8:6-8.

And God said, "Let Us make man in Our image, after Our likeness; and let them have dominion over the fish of the sea, and over the fowl of the air, and over the cattle, and over all the earth, and over every creeping thing that creepth upon the earth." So God created man in His own image, in the image of God created He him; male and female created He them. And God blessed them, and God said unto them,

"Be fruitful, and multiply, and replenish the earth, and subdue it; and have dominion over the fish of the sea, and over the fowl of the air, and over every living thing that moveth upon the earth."

A. MAN WAS CREATED BY GOD. "It is He that hath made us, and not we ourselves" (Ps. 100:3). Man shares the same mineral matter as the dust, but he is more than matter. Man is the climax of Creation, the creature for which everything else was created. Because man was created by God, he has a personal dependence on God and a responsibility to God.

B. MAN WAS CREATED IN GOD'S IMAGE. The Psalmist David described this as "a little lower than the angels" (Ps. 8:5). The Hebrew word translated "angels" is *elohim*, one of the Old Testament names for God. "For Thou hast made him a little lower than God" is an acceptable translation for the term "in God's image." This implies that man has personality like God—mind, emotions, will—and that man is basically a spiritual being. His body may, at death, return to dust, but the spirit lives on.

C. MAN WAS CREATED FOR GOD'S GLORY. When David contemplated the greatness of man, he wrote Psalm 8 to give glory to God! Twice David sang, "How excellent is Thy name in all the earth!" (vv. 1, 9). "I have created him for My glory; I have formed him; yea, I have made him" (Isa. 43:7).

D. MAN WAS CREATED AS GOD'S RULER. God crowned man and gave him dominion! It was this fact that so amazed David as he contemplated the place of man in God's vast universe. Adam became the king over God's creation, and his wife, Eve, ruled at his side.

E. MAN LOST HIS THRONE AND HIS CROWN. As long as man was ruling under the authority of God, in the will of God, and for the glory of God, everything went well. But when man went his own way, in obedience to Satan's will, then everything started to fall apart. (The familiar story is recorded in Genesis 3, and the theological explanation is given in Romans 5.) Sin marred God's image in man, and sin robbed man of God's glory: "For all have sinned, and come short of the glory of God" (Rom. 3:23). While man still has tremen- dous power in subduing creation, he creates new problems every time he makes a new discovery. He is the paradoxical combination of slave and sovereign, victor and victim!

In view of what man has done with his high and holy privileges, no wonder David was amazed that God would be mindful of him and "visitest [take note of, care for] him" (Ps. 8:4). Why would Almighty God pay any attention to sinful man? The celestial bodies obey God and give Him glory, but man disobeys God and robs Him of glory. Instead of ruling over creation, man has all but ruined creation!

Is there any hope for man? Yes, there is; and this leads us to our second king.

2. King Jesus Christ
We learned from King Adam that God the Father created us to be kings. Now we shall learn that God the Son redeemed us to be kings. The key passage is Hebrews 2:5-9,

> For He did not subject to angels the world to come, concern- ing which we are speaking. But one has testified somewhere, saying, "What is man, that Thou rememberest him? Or the son of man, that Thou art concerned about him? Thou hast made him for a little while lower than the angels; Thou hast crowned him with glory and honor, and hast appointed him over the works of Thy hands; Thou hast put all things in subjection under his feet." For in subjecting all things to him, He left nothing that is not subject to him. But now we do not yet see all things subjected to him. But we do see Him who has been made for a little while lower than the angels, namely, Jesus, because of the suffering of death crowned with glory and honor, that by the grace of God He might taste death for every one (NASB).

A. CHRIST CAME TO EARTH A MAN—THE LAST ADAM.
The first Adam came from the earth, but Jesus came down from heaven (1 Cor. 15:47). Our Lord had a real human body; He became tired, ate and drank, felt pain, and died.

But He was both God and man that He might be our Saviour.
The first Adam was tempted in a perfect paradise, and failed,
but Jesus was tempted in a horrible wilderness and was
victorious.

B. CHRIST ON EARTH EXERCISED DOMINION. This dominion was
an important part of God's mandate to Adam. Jesus had
dominion over the *animals.* He was with wild beasts in the
wilderness (Mark 1:13), and He rode on a colt on which
nobody had ever sat (Mark 11:1-7). He had dominion over
the *fowl.* Every bird in Jerusalem kept silent so that the one
cock might crow at just the right time (Luke 22:34). He
certainly had dominion over the fish! He enabled Peter and
his partners to catch a great haul of fish (Luke 5:1-11; John
21:1-6), and He even helped Peter catch *one fish* with a hook
(Matt. 17:24-27). All of nature recognized its Creator and
Lord when Jesus Christ ministered on earth.

C. CHRIST DIED TO FREE US FROM THE BONDAGE OF SIN. This
truth is expounded in Romans 5 in a series of contrasts.
Adam's sin plunged the entire human race into condemnation, sin, and death, but Christ's act of obedience—His death
on the cross—brought righteousness, salvation, and life. Because of the sin of the first Adam, sin and death reign over
mankind, but because of the righteous act of the Last Adam,
grace reigns in the lives of those who trust Him. The first
Adam was a thief and was cast out of paradise. The last Adam
turned to a thief and said, "Today shalt thou be with Me in
paradise" (Luke 23:43).

D. THROUGH JESUS CHRIST, WE REIGN AS KINGS! "But now we do
not yet see all things subjected to him [man]. But we do see
Him [Jesus]" (Heb. 2:8-9, NASB). Because of His victorious
death, resurrection, and ascension, Jesus Christ now reigns
over all things. "For He hath put all things under His feet"
(1 Cor. 15:27). The Father raised Jesus from the dead and
"put all things under His feet" (Eph. 1:22). The key verse is
Romans 5:17—"For if, by the trespass of the one man [Adam],
death reigned through that one man, how much more will
those who receive God's abundant provision of grace

and of the gift of righteousness reign in life through the one man, Jesus Christ" (NIV).

Don't lose the impact of that verse because of the complexity of the sentence, "How much more will those . . . reign in life through . . . Jesus Christ." In Jesus Christ, our lost dominion has been restored! Because of sin, death may reign all around us, but because of Christ, we can reign in life. We need not be slaves; we can live in the freedom of sovereigns! "Let not sin therefore reign in your mortal body, that ye should obey it in the lusts thereof. . . . For sin shall not have dominion over you: for ye are not under the Law, but under grace" (Rom. 6:12, 14).

When you trusted Christ as your Saviour, you were immediately identified with Him through the coming of the Holy Spirit into your life. This means that you share in His death, burial, resurrection, ascension, and coronation. God has raised us up together with Christ, and now we are seated with Him in the heavenly places (Eph. 2:4-6). Our lost dominion has been restored: "For all things are yours; whether . . . the world, or life, or death, or things present, or things to come; all are yours" (1 Cor. 3:21-22).

God the Father *created* us to be kings. This we learned from King Adam. And God the Son *redeemed* us to be kings; this we learned from King Jesus. The important question is: how do we make this work in our daily living? For the answer, we will meet our third king—King David.

3. King David

We do not know when David wrote this beautiful psalm. Some students imagine young David, the shepherd, watching over his sheep at night and marveling at God's creation. No doubt he did this often, for David was a man who saw the handiwork of God in nature.

Some students have suggested that there might be a connection between Psalm 8 and David's slaying of Goliath (1 Sam. 17). It is not difficult to see parallels between the two passages of Scripture. Goliath taunted the armies of

Israel for 40 days, and defied them to attack. David wrote "that Thou mightest still the enemy and the avenger" (Ps. 8:2). Goliath laughed at David and said he was only a youth, and David wrote that it was "out of the mouth of babes and sucklings" that God "ordained strength" (v. 2).

The Philistine threatened to give David's carcass to "the fowls of the air, and to the beasts of the field" (1 Sam. 17:44); and in Psalm 8, David rejoiced because God gave man dominion over these creatures. In Psalm 8 David gave glory to God and magnified His name; *and that was exactly why he challenged the giant!* "I come to thee in the name of the Lord of hosts, the God of the armies of Israel, whom thou hast defied" (1 Sam. 17:45). "O Lord, our Lord, how excellent is Thy name in all the earth!" (Ps. 8:9)

I am not saying that we *must* assign Psalm 8 to this event in David's life, but I am suggesting that it forms a perfect background for a personal application of this important theme of "reigning in life."

To begin with, David had already been anointed king by the Lord (1 Sam. 16:13). The Spirit of God had come upon him in power. David was not yet on his throne, and would not be for several years, but he still could exercise spiritual authority by faith. You and I, as Christians, have received the gift of the Holy Spirit, the anointing of God (1 John 2:27). We are not yet on our thrones, but we are seated with Christ on His throne, and this gives us the authority to "reign in life."

David's victory over Goliath was not the result of his size, because he was a teenager facing a man who was over 10 feet tall! Nor did David gain the victory by his own strength, for he was only a youth. Certainly his status had nothing to do with his victory, for his family was not important in Israel, and he was the youngest in the family. David won the victory because he acted like a king and depended on the divine resources God had given him when He anointed him with the Spirit.

The story of the kings is now complete. God the Father

created us to be kings, God the Son redeemed us to be kings, and God the Holy Spirit enables us to reign in life and live like kings!

All of us face "giants" in our lives—physical problems, difficult people, impossible demands, satanic attacks—and we will either conquer them or be conquered by them. We will be either victors or victims. If we depend on ourselves, we will fail, for our old nature came from King Adam, *and he was a failure.* But if we depend on Jesus Christ, through the Spirit, we will succeed.

How, then, do we "reign in life"?

To begin with, we must belong to Jesus Christ. We must be among those who have received "abundance of grace and of the gift of righteousness" (Rom. 5:17). Like David, we must have received the anointing of God through faith.

Second, we must yield ourselves to Christ. This does not mean that we "abdicate the throne" and become mere robots. Romans 5:17 states that we "reign in life by...Jesus Christ." We do it together! We are seated on His throne sharing His authority.

Third, we must depend on the Spirit of God. A full description of Romans 5:17—reigning in life—is found in Romans 6—8. We will find that the emphasis is on the power of the Spirit in the life of a yielded believer. It was the Spirit who enabled David to face the enemy bravely and defeat him completely.

Fourth, we must live for God's glory alone. After all, that is the basic emphasis of this lovely psalm—"how excellent is Thy name in all the earth!" (Ps. 8:1, 9) It is the work of the Holy Spirit to bring glory to Jesus Christ (John 16:14). While David did enjoy some special benefits from slaying the giant, his main purpose was only to glorify God.

Finally, we must trust God in the everyday needs and problems of life. Before David ever killed a giant in public, he had killed a lion and a bear in private (1 Sam. 17:32-37). The familiar song puts it perfectly:

Yield not to temptation,
For yielding is sin
Each victory will help you
Some other to win.

Psalm 8 challenges each of us to "reign in life." We have been created in God's image for God's glory. In Christ, we have regained our lost dominion *and much more* (Rom. 5:9-10, 15, 17, 20). Through the power of the indwelling Spirit, we can appropriate all the spiritual authority we need and defeat all the enemies that oppose us.

What is man?

Whatever he believes himself to be!

If he believes Satan, then man is a slave of sin. If he believes God, then man can be a king.

For some reason, when I was a boy in school, I memorized the full name of the then Duke of Windsor—Edward Albert Christian George Andrew Patrick David Windsor. He reigned as King of Great Britain and Ireland for less than one year, from January 20 to December 10, 1936. I can barely remember the excitement that spread throughout the world when King Edward VIII announced his abdication. He was giving up the throne to marry Mrs. Wallis Simpson!

Sentimentalists and traditionalists will argue until the end of time as to the rationale of his decision, and that does not concern me. What does concern me is this: when he left his throne, he gave up a great deal of wealth and authority. That is exactly what happens to believers when they do not "reign in life by . . . Jesus Christ."

Permit the three kings to share their messages again,

Adam: "God the Father created you to be a king."

Jesus Christ: "I, God the Son, redeemed you to be a king."

The Holy Spirit: "I, God the Spirit, can enable you to live like a king, and to reign in life."

There is yet one more king to be heard from—YOU!

Will you, by faith, ascend the throne with Jesus Christ and start reigning in life?

If you do, then you will soon be singing with David: "O Lord, our Lord, how excellent is Thy name in all the earth!" (v. 1, 9)

12

The Wonder of It All!

Psalm 139

¹O Lord, Thou hast searched me, and known me. ²Thou knowest my downsitting and mine uprising, Thou understandest my thought afar off. ³Thou compassest my path and my lying down, and art acquainted with all my ways. ⁴For there is not a word in my tongue, but, lo, O Lord, Thou knowest it altogether. ⁵Thou hast beset me behind and before, and laid Thine hand upon me. ⁶Such knowledge is too wonderful for me; it is high, I cannot attain unto it. ⁷Whither shall I go from Thy spirit? Or whither shall I flee from Thy presence? ⁸If I ascend up into heaven, Thou art there; if I make my bed in hell, behold, Thou art there. ⁹If I take the wings of the morning, and dwell in the uttermost parts of the sea; ¹⁰Even there shall Thy hand lead me, and Thy right hand shall hold me. ¹¹If I say, "Surely the darkness shall cover me; even the night shall be light about me." ¹²Yea, the darkness hideth not from Thee; but the night shineth as the day. The darkness and the light are both alike to Thee. ¹³For Thou hast possessed my reins. Thou hast covered me in my mother's womb. ¹⁴I will praise Thee; for I am fearfully and wonderfully made; marvelous are Thy works; and that my soul knoweth right well. ¹⁵My substance was not hid from Thee, when I was made in secret, and curiously wrought in the lowest parts of the earth. ¹⁶Thine eyes did see my substance, yet being unperfect; and in Thy book all my members were written, which in continuance were fashioned, when as yet there was none of them. ¹⁷How precious also are Thy thoughts unto me, O God! How great is the sum of them! [18]*If I should count them, they are more in number than the sand. When I awake, I am still with Thee.* [19]*Surely Thou wilt slay the wicked, O God; depart from me therefore, ye bloody men.* [20]*For they speak against Thee wickedly, and Thine enemies take Thy name in vain.* [21]*Do not I hate them, O Lord, that hate Thee? And am not I grieved with those that rise up against Thee?* [22]*I hate them with perfect hatred; I count them mine enemies.* [23]*Search me, O God, and know my heart; try me, and know my thoughts;* [24]*And see if there be any wicked way in me, and lead me in the way everlasting.*

"The fairest thing we can experience is the mysterious," wrote scientist Albert Einstein. "He who knows it not, can no longer wonder, no longer feel amazement, is as good as dead, a snuffed-out candle."

If what Einstein wrote is true, then many people are snuffed-out candles! For the most part, people have lost their sense of wonder. By nature, little children have a sense of wonder and live in a world that is governed by miracle. Then they pass through a "fantasy stage" (which is *artificial* wonder) into the cold, practical world of scientific explanations and interchanging parts. Poof! There goes wonder!

This loss of wonder is costly. For one thing, it promotes pride, because we think we can explain everything. Actually, the more that science discovers, the more wonderful creation becomes. It is only the pseudo-scientist or the person with only a smattering of learning who thinks that true science destroys a sense of wonder. All honest scholars admit their ignorance and wonder at how much there is to learn.

Our modern-day loss of wonder has helped make us shallow and hollow. Wonder and worship go together, and worship leads to depth. Wonder and worship help us put daily life into perspective, and perspective helps us determine true values. This may explain why modern society wants entertainment instead of enrichment and "a good time" rather than a good life.

One of the major themes of Psalm 139 is the wonder of God. But this psalm is not a lecture on theology. It is the record of what happens to a believer when he takes time to think on the wonder of God. In this magnificent hymn, David shares with us four wonders of God, and applies these truths to our lives.

1. The wonder of God's knowledge (vv. 1-6)

Omniscience is the theological word for God's knowledge, and it simply means that God knows everything. If God is God at all, then certainly He must know everything; otherwise, He would be a "limited God," and thus not God at all.

But the psalmist did not consider the wonder of God's knowledge in an abstract, philosophical way. He applied it to himself personally. Five times in this psalm, he stated that God knew *him* (vv. 1-2, 4, 23). God knew him because He had *searched* him. The Hebrew word means "to examine carefully, to explore."

What does God actually know about us? He knows *what we do,* our "downsittings" and "uprisings" (v. 2). This refers to the daily activities of life (Deut. 6:7). He knows *what we think,* and He knows it even before we think it! God also knows *where we go* (Ps. 139:3). The word translated "compasseth" in the *King James Version* means "to sift or winnow as grain." God knows where we go, and He passes judgment on our actions. Even when we lie down, God knows it and either approves or disapproves.

God also knows *what we say* (v. 4), and, like our thoughts, He knows our words before we speak them. God tries our hearts and knows even the motives that lie behind our words (Heb. 4:12-13). This explains why we must constantly pray, "Let the words of my mouth, and the meditation of my heart, be acceptable in Thy sight, O Lord, my strength and my redeemer" (Ps. 19:14).

Finally, God knows *what we need* (Ps. 139:5), and therefore, He keeps His guiding and restraining hand on us. "Beset" means "hemmed in like a city under siege." By His providential care, God protects and provides for us, even when we do not realize it. We are surrounded by God!

When David tried to understand the greatness of God's knowledge, he found himself overwhelmed. But this is nothing to apologize for, because wonder and worship are the proper responses to the glorious attributes of God. Paul responded in a similar way in Romans 11:33-36, and he was probably the greatest Christian theologian who ever lived. Dr. G. Campbell Morgan, the great expositor, once said, "When all of my attempts at exegesis fail, I worship." A vision of God ought to give us a burning heart, not a big head.

2. The wonder of God's presence (vv. 7-12)

The atheist wrote on the chalkboard: "GOD IS NOWHERE." But a Christian used the eraser and made a significant change, so that it read: "GOD IS NOW HERE." The theologians call this *omnipresence:* God is present everywhere at all times.

David did not feel like a prisoner, even though he was "hemmed in" by God. He felt free to travel, but he knew that he could not escape God. The fact that God knows everything and is everywhere does not turn the world into a prison. While we cannot explain completely the relationship between man's freedom and God's sovereignty, we do know as a certainty that they both exist. To know God, yield fully to Him, and do His will through life, *is* the greatest freedom.

Is it possible to go to a place where you will not find God? Jonah attempted to flee from the presence of the Lord, only to discover that God was with him to bring him back to the place of obedience and service. Our first parents attempted to hide from God, but God in His grace found them out. "'Can a man hide himself in hiding places, so I do not see him?' declares the Lord. 'Do I not fill the heavens and the earth?' declares the Lord" (Jer. 23:24, NASB).

First, David tried the heights and the depths, heaven and the underworld of the dead, and he discovered that God was present. The word translated "hell" in Psalm 139:8 of the *King James Version* is *sheol,* a Hebrew word for the realm of the dead. Throughout the Bible, the two places are contrasted. Heaven is a place of life and light, while sheol is a place of darkness and death. Yet God is in both places.

Then David decided to travel from east to west. In verse 9, he met the dawn and traveled with the sun toward "the uttermost parts of the sea." This would be the Mediterranean Sea and would be west of the Holy Land. The Jewish people, for the most part, were not mariners and did not like the sea, but God was even on the seas! God's hand would be there to lead and to protect (v. 10).

David had investigated the heights and the depths, the east and the west, and the land and the sea, and he had found no place where God was not. But, perhaps there is a difference in our experience of God's presence from day to night. No, David learned that darkness is like light to God! We cannot hide from God in the darkness.

The truth of the omnipresence of God is a most frightening one to an unbeliever but a comforting one to a Christian. No matter where we are, God is there. Our Lord is named "Immanuel . . . God with us" (Matt. 1:23). "Lo, I am with you alway" (Matt. 28:20). Even when our situation seems dark and difficult, God is there. "Fear thou not; for I am with thee; be not dismayed; for I am thy God. I will strengthen thee; yea, I will help thee; yea, I will uphold thee with the right hand of My righteousness" (Isa. 41:10).

Because God is always present with His people, we are never alone and we are never without the resources for life and ministry. If we are in the will of God, we will never lack the provision of God. It has well been said that the will of God will never lead us where the grace of God cannot keep us. It was the assurance of the presence of God that sustained the Apostle Paul in his many difficult tasks (Acts 18:1-11; 23:11; 2 Tim. 4:16-18).

3. The wonder of God's power (Ps. 139:13-18)

God is not only omniscient and omnipresent, but He is omnipotent—all-powerful. The psalmist might have used God's vast creation as an example of God's great power; but, instead, he used the miracle of birth. Conception, development, and birth are perpetual wonders that an understanding of genetics, anatomy, and obstetrics cannot erase. It is tragic that the human fetus is too often considered a nuisance to be removed, like a ruptured appendix, instead of a miracle to be admired and welcomed.

GOD IS THE AUTHOR OF LIFE. These verses make it clear that God is personally concerned with the conception, development, and birth of each child. The word "possessed" in verse 13 means "formed or created." God formed our "inward parts [reins]" and arranged our genetic structure. "Before I formed thee in the womb, I knew thee" (Jer. 1:5; and see Isa. 49:5 and Gal. 1:15). God also "covered" us in the womb, which means He "wove us together, shaped us." (The Hebrew word also can mean "protected," which shows how precious the unborn child is to the heavenly Father.)

Verses 15 and 16 of Psalm 139 are a poetical description of the development of a child in the womb. The word "substance" in verse 15 refers to the skeleton, the bony framework of the child; while in verse 16, the word is a different Hebrew word which means "an unformed mass folded together." The quaint phrase "curiously wrought" simply means "intricately made with great care." The Latin word from which we get our word "curious" simply means "wrought with care."

All of this is done in secret "in the lowest parts of the earth." This does not suggest that the baby is not formed in the mother's womb! It is poetic language for secrecy and mystery. We come from the dust of "Mother Earth," though we are formed in the mother's womb.

Verse 16 gives translators a bit of a problem, so perhaps we ought to quote a few versions:

"Your eyes saw my unformed body. All the days ordained for me were written in Your Book before one of them came to be" (NIV).

"Thine eyes beheld my unformed substance, and in Thy Book all was recorded and prepared day by day, when as yet none of them had being" (MLB).

"Thine eyes have seen my unformed substance; and in Thy Book they were all written. The days that were ordained for me, when as yet there was not one of them" (NASB).

In our *King James Version* the phrase "my members" is in italics, which means it was added by the translators and was not in the original text. Is the verse talking about the members of the body being ordained by God, or the actual days of a person's life?

I think that *both* are involved. God has made us as we are, and we must accept ourselves and be ourselves. Some people are born with many gifts and abilities, while others are perhaps less than average. We should develop what we have and use it all for God's glory. In the Parable of the Pounds (Luke 19:11-27) and the Parable of the Talents (Matt. 25:14-30), the basis for reward is not how many abilities we have, but how faithful we are to use what we have. We must never complain to God about the way we are made. Rather, we must surrender to Him and let Him use us to accomplish the purposes for which we were made.

This brings us to the second aspect of this fascinating verse: that God has ordained the days of our lives. This is not the impersonal blueprint of a distant engineer, but the loving plan of a gracious heavenly Father. First, God makes us as He wants us to be; then He plans for us a life here on earth that will best fulfill all that He put into us! The New Testament parallel is Ephesians 2:10, "For we are His workmanship, created in Christ Jesus for good works, which God prepared beforehand, that we should walk in them" (NASB).

The thinking student immediately recognizes the tremendous application of such truths to such questions as abortion, suicide, and "mercy killing." We believe life comes from God, and God supervises the growth of the fetus, therefore we have no right to interfere. If God has ordained life, man should not "play God" and start prescribing death.

What was the psalmist's response to these great truths? Grateful praise! "I will praise Thee; for I am fearfully and wonderfully made" (Ps. 139:14). Instead of crying and complaining because he was not made some other way, the writer actually gave thanks that God had fashioned him the way he was.

If God is able to create a new human being in the womb, then surely He is a great and powerful God. The fact that we have "test-tube babies" today does not mean that God has been dethroned, for men are simply imitating what God can do. If man ever does "create life" in the laboratory, it will only prove once again that it takes life to create life. God is still in control, but men had better bow before Him and obey His laws, lest they try to become God and interfere with His natural laws.

In verses 17-18, David recorded his rapture at meditating on God's thoughts toward him. It is not so much what David thought about God that stirred him but the fact that God thought about him! (See Jer. 29:11.) "How precious are Thy thoughts *concerning* me!" might be the best translation. God thinks about us even when we are not thinking about God. We go to sleep, but He never slumbers or sleeps. Apparently David went to sleep, meditating on these great truths, and he woke up thinking about the God who had been thinking about him all night.

4. The wonder of His judgment (Psalm 139:19-24)

Verses 19-22 may seem out of place in this beautiful song about the wonderful attributes of God. Are we to believe that the God who tenderly cares for the unborn baby would actually slay the wicked? How can David claim to love God and yet hate people made in the image of God?

You have probably noticed in your personal reading of the Book of Psalms that sometimes the writers express violent opposition to their enemies and ask for God's terrible judgment upon them. Such psalms as 35, 58, 59, 83, 109, and 137 are called "the imprecatory psalms" because they are characterized by this call for judgment. There are sections in other psalms that also fit into this category. How do we explain these statements, especially in the light of the Christian revelation of forgiveness?

To begin with, this attitude is not born of personal malice or vindictiveness. The psalmist saw God's enemies as his own enemies (compare 139:20 and 22). While it is good to say that we should hate sin but love the sinner, we must confess that it is the sinful sinner who commits the sin. Other people in Bible history expressed this same kind of hatred against God's enemies: Jeremiah (Jer. 11:18ff; 15:15ff; 18:19ff); the Apostle Paul (Gal. 1:8-9); and even our Lord Jesus Christ (Matt. 21:40-44; 22:7; Luke 19:27).

The alternative, of course, is to condone sin and permit wicked men and women to go unrestrained and unjudged. Modern society has such a weak view of God that they have left no room for His holy judgment against sin. Furthermore, too many Christians today have such a weak and inadequate view of sin that they have become so sentimental that they have ceased to be spiritual.

"But should we not leave such judgment to God?" the sentimentalist asks. *That is exactly what the psalmist was doing when he prayed these prayers!* He was asking God to do the work of judgment which only He could do. The psalmist's motive was the glory of God and the advancement of God's kingdom.

In some of the imprecatory psalms, we learn that the psalmist had personally tried to help these people, but they had refused his witness. (See Pss. 35:12-14 and 109:4-5.) Furthermore, these psalms indicate that the sinners being judged are only receiving the same treatment they have given to innocent people. (See Ps. 109:16-20.) Would we have God suspend His own law of sowing and reaping?

Christians are taught to pity their persecutors and to pray for them, but we live in the full light of Calvary and the teaching concerning the future judgment at the end of time. The Old Testament believer saw the holy wrath of God, not at Calvary, but in the acts of God in history. During the "childhood" of the nation of Israel (Gal. 3:19—4:7), God taught them on the basis of rewards and punishments, just as we teach our children. Now that "the fullness of the times" has come, we can see God's total plan more clearly, but this does not mean we should not hate sin and want to see it rooted out and judged. "Ye that love the Lord, hate evil" (Ps. 97:10).

Finally, we must consider the context of this expression of judgment. David had just considered the wonder of God's knowledge, presence, and power. If God has all these wonderful attributes, why is evil so successful in this world? God knows all things, and God can do all things! Yet, God seems to be doing nothing! Jeremiah had the same problem (Jer. 12:1ff) and so did Job (Job 21). As New Testament Christians, we realize that God has settled the sin problem at the cross, that He Himself has suffered for us, so that we cannot accuse Him of not doing anything. But the Old Testament believer did not have the benefit of this clear understanding.

Having said that, I must point out that "progressive revelation" in the Bible is not from the false to the true, but from lesser light to greater light. The psalmist's views of sin and judgment were not false, but neither were they complete. Because we have the Epistle to the Romans, we can understand better how God can be patient with the rebel and (seemingly) not punish sin during this Gospel age of reconciliation.

The final two verses of the psalm certainly absolve the writer of any personal vindictiveness, for he asks God to judge him! God had already searched him and known him (v. 1), but he asked for another "spiritual investigation." He had been grieved by the evil deeds of the wicked (v. 21), but he wanted to be sure that his own sins were not grieving God. (The phrase "wicked way" (v. 24) means "a way of grief.") This is a wonderful prayer: "Search me ... try me ... lead me" (vv. 23-24). Anyone who prays like this has every right to pronounce judgment against the enemies of God!

Scriptures like 1 Timothy 4 and 2 Timothy 3 make it clear that evil men will be on the increase as the present age draws to a close. As God's people, we will need a clearer vision of God if we are going to stand true to His Word. If we are caught up in the wonder of God—His knowledge, presence, and power—then we will not be afraid of His judgment. We will love that which is holy and hate that which is wicked.

How can we be afraid or worried when we belong to such a wonderful God! (The word "thoughts" in verse 23 means "anxious thoughts.") He knows everything and cannot make a mistake. He is everywhere and will not leave us or forsake us. He can do anything and is even able to deal with the wickedness of this world in His own way and His own time.

Oh, the wonder of it all!

When you add to this the wonder of His love and grace as seen in Jesus Christ, then the wonder only grows!